DECREES, DECLARES & PRAYERS

2ND EDITION

CAROLINE GREEN

▲ ELEVITA MEDIA

Decrees, Declares & Prayers
2ND EDITION

Caroline Green

For more information on Caroline Green please visit CarolineGreen.org

Copyright © 2016 Caroline Green

The bible verses used came from King James Version, New King James Version, Amplified Version, English Standard Version, and The Message Bible.

Cover Design: Wayne Coster Cooper & Caroline Green. Production: elevitamedia.com

Printed in the United States of America Second Edition

1 2 3 4 5 6 7 8 9 10

REVIEWS

"*Decrees, Declares & Prayers* is a testament to the promises of God. The book is easy to read and builds upon your faith. It helps me get through the day."
    — **Verdree Parham-Boston, Massachusetts**

"Completing the 100-day challenge set by Caroline Green in *Decrees, Declares and Prayers* positively transformed my thoughts and actions. Lifting my voice to God daily with passages from this devotional kept my heart and mind on His Word, His glory, and His goodness."
    — **Stephanie Sommerville-Invercargill, New Zealand**

"*Decrees, Declares & Prayers* is a 'Must Have' for any Believer. Caroline reminds us the power of God's Word and how speaking that Word in our life can change our life. Truly needed in the Body of Christ."
    — **Yvette E. Clark, Exhortation Corner Ministries-Conyers, GA**

"Caroline Green shows us new things about the power of the tongue. She also teaches us how we can speak our highest expectations into the important areas of our lives—all for the glory and with the blessing of God. *Decrees, Declares & Prayers* is an excellent resource for living."
    — **Wayne Coster Cooper, WritersInTheSpirit-Charlotte, NC**

"Occasionally, we may need to be reminded of powerful scriptures and how they can transform how we think, feel, and the necessity to take on the armor of God's goodness. When I read Caroline Green's *Decrees, Declares & Prayers* it reassured me of God's great promises, while renewing my faith over and over again. Thank you Caroline!"
    — **Dr. Crystal Green Brown, Health & Life Coach-Charlotte, NC**

The Lord God has given me the tongue of the learned, that I should know how to speak a word in season to him who is weary. He awakens me morning by morning, He awakens my ear to hear as the learned.

Isaiah 50:4

I dedicate this book to all believers everywhere. Empower life with the words of your mouth!

CREATE POWERFUL BREAKTHROUGHS

The Greatest Physical Weapon God Gave Us Is Our Mouths

CONTENTS

WHY I WROTE THIS BOOK

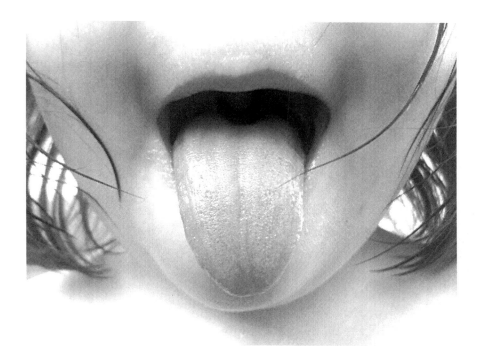

The tongue has the power of life and death.

Proverbs 18:21

**Thou shalt also decree a thing,
and it shall be established unto thee:
and the light shall shine upon thy ways.**

Job 22:28

My son, give attention to my words;
Incline your ear to my sayings.
Do not let them depart from your eyes;
Keep them in the midst of your heart;
For they are life to those who find them,
and health to all their flesh.

Proverbs 4:20-22

For the word of God is quick, and
powerful, and sharper than any
twoedged sword, piercing even to the
dividing asunder of soul and spirit,
and of the joints and marrow,
and is a discerner of the thoughts
and intents of the heart.

Hebrews 4:12

Let your speech be always with grace,
seasoned with salt, that ye may know
how ye ought to answer every man.

Colossians 4:6

Keep your heart with all diligence,
for out of it spring the issues of life.

Proverbs 4:23

Every man is master of his own house;
whatever he says, goes.

Esther 1:22

Let the words of my mouth and
the meditation of my heart be
acceptable in Your sight, O LORD,
my strength and my Redeemer.

Psalm 19:14

Your word I have hidden in my heart,
That I might not sin against You.

Psalm 119:11

Today I have given you the choice
between life and death, between
blessings and curses. Now I call
on heaven and earth to witness the
choice you make. Oh, that you
would choose life, so that you and
your descendants might live!

Deuteronomy 30:19

For verily I say unto you, that whosoever shall say unto this mountain, be thou removed, and be thou cast into the sea; and shall not doubt in his heart, but shall believe that those things which he saith shall come to pass; he shall have whatsoever he saith.

Mark 11:23

When I read these verses, I saw a pattern of principles and asked myself, "do you see the running theme in these verses?" I then began to compile my knowledge of the Word of God and remembered that I had read, "we reap what we sow." Other interpretations I heard used from different people were based on when someone did something bad or evil. Statements like, "Karma," and "what goes around, comes around," were often made.

I started to think about what if I were to take action on a daily basis to speak and proclaim out loud the opposite of the perceived negative circumstances I was facing. Would a more desirable lifestyle and walk with the Lord come to pass? Would I behave more like Christ Jesus towards others and myself? Then I grappled with the thoughts of "is this realistic and logical?" How can I honestly deny what I see happening?

Seriously, for example, how could I speak the opposite of not being able to afford something when clearly I did not have the money to make the purchase to begin. I am talking about sensible items here such as necessity items. Would this be some kind of insane notion, non-reality, or fantasy world that I would create? Well, as it turns out the answer is no.

Please understand this is way beyond the power of money and purchasing abilities. It is not about denying what we see or feel, it is about knowing and speaking the Word of God, His promises out loud by faith, believing and trusting God at His Word on a daily basis throughout a believers life time.

I also considered that if I reap what I sow then why wouldn't I be better off by sowing positive, life giving words, and speaking the Word of God by faith through decrees, declares, and prayer petitions to watch my atmosphere, circumstances, and perceptions change? To see my own self changed for the better, obviously could not hurt. Habakkuk 2:4 tells us the just shall live by his or her faith. I made a choice to believe this word for word.

Furthermore, I thought about if I were to put into action what I read in those scriptures then the quality of my perceptions could possibly improve the quality of my circumstances over time. My perceptions would be optimistic, my faith and trust in God would strengthen, increasing daily over the course of time. Understand that the Word of God is powerful and alive.

Since faith comes by hearing and hearing the Word of God, it makes sense to decree a thing using my tongue to speak life-giving words and pray scriptures out loud. I understood according to Ephesians 6:12 that my battles were not with flesh and blood, but my battles were in the spirit realm.

In my quest to know more, I began to research available science and look for the possibilities of clinical trials performed of how words spoken out loud affect the physical body over time. I also was interested in finding out how this could affect one's circumstances. I believe in the Word of God because I have personally experienced His truth in my own life. No one can dismiss a person's personal experiences.

However, I was still curious of learning about any scientific findings. So, I did some research and what I found was impressive to say the least; scientists proved that emotions are embedded on a person's DNA. They also proved that a person could change their DNA through words and verbal frequencies.

Everything has an energy field and gives off vibrations, or frequencies in scientific terms. **<u>Therefore, the words we speak give off energy, which over time creates the unseen things in our lives.</u>**

Hebrews 11:1 is really a profound piece of divine knowledge supporting science. Better yet, science supports the Word of God! The scripture says that, "Now faith is the substance of things hoped for, the evidence of things not seen." If you actually meditate and deeply consider what Hebrews 11:1 is saying, this one verse will change the way you trust God, perceive your circumstances, think about your life, think about how you speak out of your mouth, and behave toward others.

Our life will change over time IF WE CONTINUE AND BE CONSISTENT in the things and teachings of what God's Word instructs. Having a "teachable heart" at all times is necessary in order to apply God's principles and character traits in our lives.

This devotional reference book was written by a believer of Christ Jesus. The intent of writing this book was to shine a light for other believers who may, or may not have faith in God, lack understanding of the power, importance, and the effect words spoken out loud over any type of situation bears on one's life. In addition, most believers are so loose and careless with their speech not realizing the consequences of what they are saying and how negative they really speak about themselves or others.

I want believers to have knowledge of what to say and how to make declarations praying effectively over their lives and others.

More importantly, one of the main reasons the Lord led me

to write this book was to point out to all the believers and myself about the negativity we each speak out of our mouths on a daily basis either about ourselves, our lives, our situations, and about others. It is not walking and speaking by faith when we are negative.

Negativity creates discouragement resulting in failures, delays, set backs, and distress. We are to live by faith and by every word that comes from the mouth of God. His Word brings life. Hebrews 10:38, a precursor to Hebrews 11:1 reminds us, "the just shall live by faith."

In the book of Job chapter 38, God made a series of challenges to Job and in verses 12 and 13 God made a very insightful statement. God asked Job had he ever commanded his morning since his days had begun and cause the dawn to know its place that it might take hold of the ends of the earth so the wicked would be shaken out of it. That is the power God has and as a born again believer in Christ Jesus we have been equipped with God's power to simply stand in faith and speak the Word of God expecting it to manifest. Our words are powerful!

This book is to be used as a reference guide to encourage you to read it more than once, pointing you directly to the Word of God concerning numerous areas of life we all face at one time or another. I decree, declare and pray that you, the readers will grow in the knowledge of God's Word, principles, and character in the mighty name of Jesus! Amen!

WHY YOU SHOULD READ THIS BOOK

Thou shalt also decree a thing, and it shall be established unto thee: and the light shall shine upon thy ways.

Job 22:28

Job 22:28 states that when thou (you) decree a thing it shall be established and the light shall shine upon thy (your) ways. Get a hold of the interpretation of what this scripture is saying: you speak a thing, and it will come to pass, and the light shall shine on your ways. Who's ways will light shine on? Your ways, your outcome of what you spoke and decreed. We get exactly what we speak and the light will shine on those outcomes. If you call yourself stupid or your child stupid, your words will create actions, choices, decisions of stupidity in yourself or your child. Those actions, choices, and decisions will be lit up by the light being revealed on the way (outcome).

Therefore, decree, declare, and pray out loud the Word of God as much as possible on a daily basis. If you don't know what to say use this book to bridge the gap until you learn the scriptures. I have done the research and work by compiling many decrees, declares and prayers with references scriptures addressing numerous things we all face as believers. To speak these out loud, will go against what your flesh wants to do, but you will get whatever you speak. You might as well speak life-giving words. So pry your mouth open, start praising God, start decreeing, declaring, and praying out loud. Watch and see a spirit of exhortation come upon you!

From the fruit of his mouth, a man's stomach is filled; with the harvest from his lips, he is satisfied. (Proverbs 18:20)

You are going to be filled with what you SPEAK!

Jesus called the crowd to himself and said, "Listen and understand. What goes into a man's mouth does not make him unclean, but what comes out of his mouth, that is what makes him unclean." (Matthew 15:10-11) The things that come out of the mouth come from the heart. (Matthew 15:18)

As a reminder, I have written this book as an easy supplemental devotional reference guide that is intended to accompany the reader in his or hers daily biblical study time.
Additionally, it is to assist in changing what you are thinking and speaking daily, so you will live as more than a conqueror already provided by Christ Jesus.

The majority of the decrees, declares, and prayers are straight out of the scriptures. I have added additional specific prayers in this second edition that tackle a wide range of topics in order to further help the saints. Prayer is a mighty weapon that should be used daily to advance the kingdom of God and tear down the enemy from advancing any further in your life as well as others. Jesus prayed daily to the Father in Heaven. He is our example to follow.

These decrees, declares, and prayers are intended to be spoken out loud to increase your faith and bring awareness of watching your own words that come out of your mouth. You speak it and believe what it says. Then go read the actual scriptures with each one.

My desire is for Christians to stop with the negative talk, speak the Word standing in faith while believing it in their hearts. We all need to be reminded, reprimanded, and made aware of what God's Word says about the words we choose to let come our of our mouths. Furthermore, how those words shape our destinies and the generation that follows. Our words are powerful, so we all need to practice discipline in speaking life giving words.

The Word of God says that faith comes by hearing and hearing the Word of God. (Romans 10:17) Make the decision today that you will decree, declare and pray God's Word out loud over yourself and others as a daily routine. God wants us prosperous in our souls (mind, will, and emotions). God wants His children to trust Him and be obedient to follow His principles and character. The joy of the Lord is our strength. (Nehemiah 8:10) Get happy and rejoice because happy people spread joy, love, kindness, hope, and good will.

Understand that positive thinking is helpful, but speaking the Word of God, mixed with your faith while praying out loud engaging your mouth to speak life, faith, love, kindness, and thoughtful words is where the power resides.

<u>I challenge you to intentionally</u> use words in this book and/or create your own decrees, declares, and prayers for your use <u>over the next 100 days</u> as a test to the validity of changes to come in your mind, body, soul, spirit, and experiences.

As you begin this journey, you will notice that changes and challenges will go hand in hand over the course of this process. There will be days of great achievements, breakthroughs, and enormous change as God uses your mouth, words from your tongue, to create your thoughts and beliefs. You will increase your faith in His Words, strength, abilities, and promises. Continue to stand on the Word of God.

You will create new improved pathways in your physical brain. Science has proven this, more importantly; God designed our brains to function in His likeness. God's Word does not return void (Isaiah 55:11). We are created in the image and likeness of God (Genesis 1:26-27) and scripture states that death and life are in the power of the tongue (Proverbs 18:21). These are scriptures worth understanding as you read this book daily. God also provides another golden nugget in scripture to "choose life so you and your children may live." (Deuteronomy 30:19)

This book is laid out as a reference guide with chapters titled for the "wheel of life" situations we all face. To further equip your understanding of God's Word, be sure to **include reading out loud the actual bible verses referenced** from your own bible that are with each of the decrees, declares and prayers.

For this Second Edition I have included more scriptures, and specific prayers. So get your bibles out and get to work. You may notice that there is some repetitiveness in this book, which proves that God's Word and speaking it can cover all your circumstances. Just go with the flow, it is for your own good and God's glory to happen in your life.

I decree, declare, and pray that as you read this book and the scriptures you will increase in the knowledge of God in every area of your life in the name of Jesus! Amen!

MY TESTIMONY

My testimony has really taken shape over the last few years once I got fed up with being ineffective in life and in spiritual matters (they are directly connected). I truly desired the victory over sin, shortcomings, poverty, carnality, and negativity. As I look back I realize I want everything God said I could have according to His Word. I want to be who God wants me to be, not what I want to be. Being defeated, living defeated, thinking defeated thoughts, speaking like a defeated child of God are all an oxymoron.

I want to hear God say to me, "well done good and faithful servant, enter My rest." I realized that my decisions directly determined my rewards, but in order to be rewarded I was going to have to step out of my comfort zone and get away from things of familiarity. To take action was solely up to me. I had to change the company I kept and the personal influences I allowed to be in my life. I had to change my words, I had to contradict my traditional self. I had to change where I was attending church. I had to change what I listened to, what I watched, and what I gave my attention to on a daily basis. Did this happen overnight? Of course not! However, the process began once I accepted, believed, and decided to act on God's revealed truth—so change started with the words of my tongue.

If words were not powerful to create change, and be a catalyst for good or evil, then God would have omitted Proverbs 18:21 that states, "death and life are in the power of the tongue." We would have never read of the verbal battle between Jesus and Satan in Matthew chapter four where Jesus spoke "it is written" and "it is written that man shall not live by bread alone but by every word that proceeds out of the mouth of God."

In addition, James 5:16 states that, "...the effectual fervent prayers of a righteous man availeth much." Or Job 22:28 that says, "you shall decree a thing and it shall be established unto you, and the light shall shine upon thy ways." If it weren't true than those words and statements would not have been placed in the bible. Neither would this book have been written. Science even proves God's Word to be true and accurate.

Lastly, these prayers along with the decrees and declares I have prayed over myself and others. I am this book. I have witnessed and experienced God in ways unimaginable. These are all very effective decrees, declares, and prayers lining up with the scriptures. I personally did the research compiling a biblical approach for verbal confessions and I wanted to share this knowledge with other believers for encouragement and exhortation purposes only.

If you truly desire more of God, His presence, His ways, His character, His principles, and His will for your life, then start speaking the Word, build your knowledge up of God's promises in your memory bank (your mind). Allow yourself to totally surrender to God and see the salvation of the Lord in every area of your life. It all starts with our tongues!

PRAYER FOR PERSONAL SALVATION

If you have never accepted Jesus Christ as your Lord and Savior, here is a divine appointment to pray this prayer out loud right now and make Jesus Lord over your life.

Dear Heavenly Father,

I confess and admit that I am a sinner. I repent for my sins right now. I need You! I need Your forgiveness, salvation, and deliverance. I believe that You sent Your one and only son Jesus Christ to the world and that He died in my place paying the price for my sins and has risen from the grave, seated now at Your right hand in heaven. Lord Jesus, I ask that You come into my heart and save me, deliver me from my sins and become the Lord of my life. I give my heart to You now. I thank You Lord for saving me and delivering me from hell in Jesus name I pray. Thank You Lord God and Amen!

If you have prayed this prayer for the first time, please pray ask God to place you in a spiritually balanced, good bible based teaching church and to build your spirit up in His Word and knowledge of Him.

It is critically important to surround yourself with godly, faithful, moral, positive people on a consistent basis. It is also imperative to spend time alone with God's Word reading your bible daily. God commanded Joshua after Moses passed in Joshua 1:8 to "meditate day and night, observe all that was in the Book of the Law." King David wrote in Psalms 119:105, "Thy word is a lamp unto my feet, and light unto my path." In our busy world, everything is after your attention. Discern what distracts you from fellowshipping with God daily and make the necessary changes needed. Do not waste God's time or your own time. Make certain that your primary focus is building yourself in the knowledge of God through the reading of His Word, the Holy Bible.

I promise you, if you will do these things building up your spirit with the knowledge of God and His Word, you will be encouraged and God will open a whole new world of greatness unto you. Use this book along with your daily reading of the Word of God and watch God work in your behalf. He is AWESOME like that!

PRAYER TO BRING GRUDGES TO LIGHT

Dear Heavenly Father,

I am checking my heart for any grudges that may be hidden. I am asking the Holy Spirit to bring any to light—exposing them now in order to open me up fully to be forgiven by You completely in the name of Jesus.

Jesus, I let go of all grudges, aggravations, frustrations, ill will, revenge, hatred, bitterness, pain, hurt, resentfulness, and all unforgiveness I have in my heart towards _____. I choose to release _____ from any and all debts, obligations, broken commitments, misplaced responsibilities, and lack of accountability due to me from him/her in the mighty name of Jesus I pray.

Dear Lord God, I purposely renounce any and all agreements I had knowingly and unknowingly with Satan's will to hold grudges and unforgiveness in my heart against _____. I release _____ to Your will and care in Jesus name.

Lord I thank You for forgiving me of my own sins completely and requiring me to do the same for others who have hurt me and done me wrong. Please remind me that my own actions to forgive others continually while removing and renouncing grudges will allow my own prayers to be answered. I pray that Your will be done on earth as it is in heaven concerning me and _____ in Jesus name I pray. Amen!

(Reference Scriptures: Matthew 18:21-35, Mark 11:12-14 and verses 20-25)

PRAYER FOR GOD TO SAVE OTHERS

In Matthew 12:29 and in Matthew 9:38 Jesus shared some seriously powerful knowledge with keen insight. He made a statement in Matthew 12:29 concerning the strongman. Jesus said "to first bind the strongman and then enter his house and spoil his goods." Jesus also advised his disciples in Matthew 9:38 "pray therefore the Lord of the harvest, that he will send out laborers into His harvest."

Put together these powerful statements that Jesus shared, pray the Word out loud, then you will see the victory in those people you are interceding for if you will continue to pray for them in faith believing God for the out come.

So pray out loud the prayer below over others by placing their name in the blanks. Do not sit by and let the devil take people without a fight.

Pray use the authority that Jesus Christ has given you as a believer! Come against the god of this world, which is Satan (2 Corinthians 4:3-4), take the blinders off their eyes and open their minds to the truth, which is the light of the glorious gospel of Christ, so they can be set free.

PRAY THIS SALVATION PRAYER OVER OTHERS:

You evil and unclean spirit thwarting the destiny and blinding the spiritual eyes of _____, upon the power and authority of the Lord Jesus Christ I command you to stop what you are doing to keep _____ out of the kingdom of God, right now in the name of Jesus! I cancel all your power and authority over _____. Dear Heavenly Father, please send someone to _____ with the Word of God.

I believe, standing in faith that I receive _____ salvation and deliverance. I praise You for it to be done according to Your Word Lord. I praise You Lord God for the good report! It's in the mighty name of Jesus I pray this prayer. Amen!

A GREAT DAILY PRAYER

Here is an example of a great daily prayer to memorize as a soldier of God.

I decree, declare, and pray that I am the head and not the tail, above only and not beneath. I am blessed going out, blessed going in, and I am daily loaded down with benefits. I am highly favored of the Lord. A host of His angels have been given charge over me keeping me in all my ways and no weapon formed against me shall prosper in the name of Jesus.

I cancel all of Satan's plans, plots, or actions and all his hosts' plans that are assigned against me and my family in the name of Jesus. I claim the protection of the blood of Jesus. According to the Word of God, Satan and his hosts are under my feet in Jesus name.

I have the victory and I walk in victory in Jesus name! Amen!

PRAYER FOR GOD TO INCREASE YOUR BOLDNESS

Dear Heavenly Father,

You are God, who made heaven and earth and sea, and all that is in them. You created our universe. Everything and every person does whatever Your hand, Your purpose, and Your counsel determined before to be done. Now Lord God, look on the threats of my enemies and Your enemies and grant to me Your servant that with all boldness I may speak Your Word by stretching forth Your hand to heal, and that signs and wonders may be done by the name of Your holy child and servant Jesus.

Heavenly Father, I don't care what the devil and his hosts say, I'm not going to back down. I am going to keep on talking and living by faith and I am going to do it boldly. Please turn up Your power on me and give me great grace to stay the course and press for the prize in the mighty name of Jesus I pray! Hallelujah! Thank You Lord God! Amen!

(Read Acts 4:5-33)

PRAYER FOR GOD TO SEND
A HIGHER-RANKING ANGEL

In Daniel Chapter 10 verses 12 and 13 we understand that the angel explained to Daniel that he had come after his words but the prince of the kingdom of Persia withstood (strong resistance or opposition) him 21 days as he was alone there until Michael, one of the chief princes came to help him so he could get to Daniel the understanding needed for the visions that Daniel had previously.

This gives us a look into the spiritual dimension as to why there was a delay in getting his prayer answered. Now Daniel would know how to pray differently in the future and so should we as believers of the Word of God.

Therefore, if you have been seeking God, perhaps fasting along with being in prayer, really searching for understanding concerning things connected to your life whether it's people, visions, dreams, ministry, work, career, family, directions, instructions, or discernment;

Then this prayer may help, but remember that God has His timing and we are instructed to wait patiently on Him. However, there is no harm in asking God for extra help.

HERE'S THE PRAYER:

Dear Heavenly Father,

You know all things and You order my steps. You know everything about me and what I need and when I need it. (Psalms 139:1-6) Lord God if there is any angelic warfare preventing You from answering my prayer request, then would You please send a higher-ranking angel now to release the angel that is bringing my answer or my understanding of the matter.

I ask this in the mighty name of Jesus I pray. Thank You Lord God for Your mercy, grace, loving-kindness, and favor towards me concerning this prayer request.

Amen!

A DAILY WARFARE PRAYER

Dear Heavenly Father,

I bow down in worship and praise before You today. I cover myself with the blood of Jesus Christ and claim the protection of the blood for myself, my family, my finances, my home, my spirit, soul, and body. I surrender myself completely in every area of my life to You dear Lord. I take a stand against all the workings of the devil that would try to hinder me and my family from best serving You. I address myself only to the true and living God, and refuse any involvement of Satan in my prayers.

Satan I command you and all your evil hosts, forces of darkness, in the name of Jesus Christ to leave my presence now. I bring the blood of Jesus Christ between the devil and my family, my home, my finances, my spirit, soul and body. I decree and declare that Satan and his wicked spirits are subject to me in the name of the Lord Jesus Christ. Furthermore, in my own life today I destroy and tear down all the strongholds of Satan and smash the plans of Satan that have been formed against me and my family.

I tear down the strongholds of the devil against my mind, and I surrender my mind to You, Blessed Holy Spirit. I affirm, Heavenly Father, that You have not given me the spirit of fear, but of the power, and of love, and of a sound mind (2 Timothy 1:7). Therefore, I resist the spirit of fear in the name of Jesus, the Son of the true Living God, and I refuse to fear, refuse to doubt, refuse to worry because I have authority, Your power, over all the power of the enemy and nothing shall by any means hurt me (Luke 10:19).

I claim complete and absolute victory in the name of Jesus and I bind the devil and command him to loose my peace, my joy, my hope, my healing, my faith, my prosperity, and every member of my family for the glory of God and by faith I call it done!

I break and bind strongholds of Satan formed against my emotions today and I give my emotions to You, Blessed Holy Spirit. I destroy the strongholds of Satan formed against my will today. I give my will to You, Blessed Holy Spirit and I choose to make the right decisions of faith. I break the strongholds of Satan against my body today and I give my body to You, Blessed Holy Spirit, realizing that I am the temple of the Holy Ghost (1 Corinthians 3:16-17, 1 Corinthians 6:19-20).

Again, I cover myself with the blood of the Lord Jesus Christ and pray that the Holy Ghost would bring all the work of the ascension of the Lord Jesus Christ into my life today. I surrender my life and possessions to You Lord God. I refuse to fear, worry, or be discouraged in the name of Jesus. I will not hate, envy or show any type of bitterness toward my brothers, sisters, or my enemies, but I will love them with the love of God shed abroad in my heart by the Holy Ghost (Romans 5:5).

Open my eyes and show me the areas of my life that do not please You Lord and give me strength, grace, and wisdom to remove any sin or weight that would prevent our close fellowship. Work in me to cleanse me from all ground that would give the devil a foothold against me.

I claim in every way the victory of the cross over all satanic forces in my life. I pray in the name of the Lord Jesus Christ with thanksgiving and I welcome all the ministry of the Holy Spirit now. Thank You Lord God! Amen!

(Anon. 2012)

THE LORD'S PRAYER

Our Father which art in heaven, Hallowed be Thy name.

Thy kingdom come, Thy will be done in earth, as it is in heaven.

Give us this day our daily bread.

And forgive us our debts, as we forgive our debtors.

And lead us not into temptation, but deliver us from evil:

For Thine is the kingdom, and the power, and the glory, forever. Amen.

(Taken from Matthew 6:9-13 in the King James Version.)

PRAYER FOR SANCTIFICATION & STRENGTH

Dear Heavenly Father,

As Your Word says in 2 Corinthians 6:17 that as believers and of the body of Christ Jesus we are to come out from among them in the world and be separate. We are not to touch unclean things and You will receive us.

In order for me to be able to stand apart and overcome any destructive habits and not be like everyone else in the world; Father God, I ask that You sanctify me and help me separate myself from the world and all destructive habits as well as separate myself unto Your things.

In Jesus name, I ask in faith, believing in You. Jesus said in John 17:17 "that You sanctify by Your truth, and Your Word is truth."

So, dear Heavenly Father, I ask that You would strengthen me and help me to spend time in Your Word daily for my own perfecting, washing, cleansing, and renewal of my mind, in the mighty name of Jesus I pray this prayer over my life.

Thank You Lord God and Amen!

PRAYER FOR UNBELIEF & DOUBT

Dear Heavenly Father,

Your Word says that it's impossible to please You if I have any unbelief or doubt in my heart. I must believe in my heart and make confession with my mouth.

Dear Lord, I repent for not believing in You and for doubting You. Please forgive me in Jesus name I pray. Lord God, please increase my faith, help me to overcome all unbelief and doubt that I have concerning the matter of _____.
Open my eyes to receive Your truth, renew my mind to Your precepts. Please give me wisdom, understanding, insight, knowledge, and discernment about _____ in the name of Jesus I pray. Amen!

(Reference Scriptures: Mark 9:24, Mark 11:24, Romans 10:10, Hebrews 11:6, James 1:5)

PRAYERS FOR SPIRITUAL LEADERS

Dear Heavenly Father,

I thank You for _____. I thank You for allowing him/her to minister to me, sowing Your Word and truth into my life and my family. I lift up _____ to You today. I ask that You strengthen, encourage, heal, and restore virtue back to him/her. I pray that You keep _____ safe. Keep his/her family safe.

I ask that You place a hedge of protection around _____. I ask that You provide traveling mercies for him/her. I ask that You keep his/her character and reputation from being damaged. I pray that You help _____ to be able to stand up against any temptations, persecutions, or attacks that come his/her way.

I ask that You help and give him/her a strong desire and sincere motivation to walk uprightly before You at all times. I ask that You fill him/her with Your love, knowledge, wisdom, understanding, and give him/her strong discernment in all things concerning him/her personally and his/her ministry.

Surround _____ with strong intercessors and prayer warriors at all times. Please bring all the necessary resources and support to him/her both personally and for the work of the ministry. Give him/her people who are committed to the vision and mission of _____ ministry that You have called into being.

Strengthen and encourage those people that are committed

to the tasks at hand to support the ministry and the works of the ministry. Help _____ to minister true to the Word of God and operate accurately in the Gifts of the Holy Spirit at all times.

I pray that You keep his/her mind, will, and emotions in tack at all times. I ask that You pour out Your abundant blessings on _____ and his /her family. I ask that You increase _____ faith. I ask that You pour Your truth out on him/her and continue to sanctify him/her.

I pray that You answer the prayers that _____ has before You. I ask that You would send Your ministering angels to minister to him/her now, helping with whatever may be troubling or pressing on him/her today. I ask that You meet every need quickly concerning _____ ministry and the work that You have called him/her to fulfill.

I ask that You meet every need and desire in _____ personal life, home life, family affairs, and any businesses, or work related issues or situations that are before You Lord God.

I ask that You bless and restore joy to _____relation- ships with his/her family members whether those are with his/her spouse, children, parents, or siblings. Draw them all closer to You Lord God. Keep Satan and his hosts, the enemy of their souls far away.

I ask that You help _____ resist the enemy in the areas that he/she is weak and vulnerable towards. I ask that You keep _____ from sexual impurities, lust of the eyes,

lust of the flesh, greed, foolishness, and all forms of pride. I pray that You help him/her remain humble, grateful, and appreciative.

I ask that You keep _____ health in great working order. Help and remind him/her to take care of the body You gave him/her. Please keep him/her safe and guard _____ from all sicknesses and diseases. Keep him/her safe and protected from all bacteria, viruses, cancers, radiation exposures, known and unknown infirmities that would work to destroy and break down his/her body and organs.

Do the same for _____ spouse and children. Quicken his/her body and strengthen him/her today. I lift up the wife/husband today asking that You help him/her to walk with You every day. Keep _____ wife/husband safe, healthy, and trustworthy. I ask that You answer the prayers that are before You that concern the spouse. Keep their children safe and from harm. Help their children to know You in Your fullness and to walk uprightly before You all the days of their lives.

Please meet and go beyond every financial need that they each have today and in their future. Dear Lord, I thank You and I praise You that You hear my prayers, my requests and You delight in the prosperity of Your dear saints. I thank You, I stand in faith and belief that You are answering these prayer requests for_____ and all that concerns his /her life.

It's in the mighty name of Jesus I make these prayers and requests known to You, lifting up each word for You to fulfill them this day. Thank You Heavenly Father for all that You do for us! I bless You and I bless Your Holy Name! In Jesus name. Amen!

(Reference Scriptures: Psalms 103:20-22, Mark 11:24, Romans 13:1, Galatians 6:6, 1 Thessalonians 5:12-13, 1 Timothy 2:1-4, 1 Timothy 5:17-18, Hebrews 13:7, Hebrews 13:17)

PRAYERS FOR MISSIONARIES
AND MISSION WORKS

Dear Heavenly Father,

I lift up all the missionaries and those that are doing mission work across the world. I stand and touch in agreement with Your will and their prayer requests right now. Please encourage and strengthen each one right now Lord God. Help them to trust You fully and deliver them from all their fears. I pray that You keep them safe and place a hedge of protection around each of them, their family members, their ministries, and those that work along side of them.

Encamp Your ministering angels around them Lord God. Keep them safe from the attacks, snares, and ambushes of the enemy and evil people. Protect their physical and mental health. Protect the quality of their housing, clothing, food, and water. Extend the life of their material possessions and food.

According to Ephesians 3:20 You are able to go beyond what one thinks, or imagines according to Your power that works in us. Increase Your power in those doing mission work and the missionaries working to spread the Gospel wherever they may be today. Increase Your presence in their lives and in the territories, You have assigned to them. I ask that You please go beyond the financial scope of their needs by sending them the financial resources, products, materials, supplies, support, and people they each need personally, and what they need to fulfill the work of the ministry.

I ask that You please assist them greatly when encountered

with those living in impoverished and highly distressed situations. Give them abundant peace, strong discernment, witty ideas, and creative inventions when needed Lord God. Empower these mission workers and missionaries from on high Father God to set captives free and to heal broken hearts as they go out ministering the Gospel and making disciples of men and women throughout their assigned regions.

Empower each of them to minister Your Word in truth and operate accurately in the gifts of the Holy Spirit at all times. Give them extreme favor and traveling mercies at all times whether on foot, bicycles, boats, ships, vehicles, buses, trains, wagons, helicopters, or planes. Bless and favor whatever modes of transportation they are subjected to use in all situations.

Protect them and all who travel with them from ill-will people, dangerous storms, wild beasts, dangerous insects and pestilence. Bless their coming and going at all times. Increase their joy, hope, faith, love, boldness, and strength. Increase their knowledge, wisdom, and understanding of You Lord God and Your purpose. Comfort their hearts and keep their minds. Help each of them to pursue peace and holiness. Protect and guard them and each of their family members as well as co-workers from becoming defiled by any root of bitterness.

Give them each strong awareness from Your Divine supernatural abilities to understand times and seasons as well as sense any form of dangers in order to keep themselves and those they serve protected and safe at all times.

I thank You and praise You for hearing and answering these requests and supplications in the mighty name of Jesus

I pray.

Amen!

(Reference Scriptures: Deuteronomy 8:3-4, Deuteronomy 29:5, Psalms 23, Psalms 34, Psalms 37:23-29, Psalms 91, Psalms 103:20-22, Psalms 121:8, Psalms 139, Matthew 5:13-16, Matthew 28:18-20, Mark 11:24, Mark 16:15, Luke 4:18-19, John 3:16, John 14:12, John 15:16, Romans 10:14-15, Romans 12:1-2, Ephesians 1:1-23, Ephesians 3:20-21, 2 Timothy 2:7, Hebrews 11:1, Hebrews 12:14-15, Hebrews 13:1-3 and 5-6, James 1:1-6)

PRAYERS FOR GOVERNMENT
AND ELECTED OFFICIALS

Dear Heavenly Father,

Your Word says that I am to pray for those who are in authority over me, give thanks for all, live peaceable, godly, and respectably. Therefore, I pray for those in elected positions that make laws, rules, policies, procedures and create ordinances that Your Righteous cause may be glorified and at the forefront of all their decisions whether they abide in You or not.

I pray that Your will be done in and through them for the betterment of Your saints and serve the intentions of Your will in every area of service, decree, judgment, law, order, policy, ruling, ordinance, and procedure. I ask that You give them wisdom, the principle thing, discernment, and understanding in their thinking and final decision making that affects the lives of those they are elected to serve and govern.

Give them witty ideas, creative inventions, and new ways of governing our counties, cities, states, and nation that will produce spiritual blessings, blessings of economic growth and sustain generations to come in every area as well as please You and Your will.

Help them individually and corporately to further Your will and kingdom on earth as it is in heaven. I pray that if any are lost, that You would save and deliver them as well as save their whole household. I pray that You help them fend off pride, greed, and lust that would destroy any good You want them to produce for Your glory and the good of the people they serve.

Keep them safe and protect their families and investments. Keep them humble as You are the one who rises up and tears down according to Your good pleasure. Further the cause of the godly and remove the ungodly leaders as You deem fit.

Protect and bless Your saints and the innocent children who are under the rule of all elected officials, those in government, and public leadership positions. Thank You for Your mercy and grace being poured out on those in these positions as well as those living under their authority in any capacity.

Please grant repentance, bring to memory any and all wrong doing, and allow forgiveness to flow. Expose snares and traps from enemies and those that wish to do any of us harm. I ask that You protect those that serve and govern us at all times. Protect their families and loved ones. May You always be glorified and Your righteous cause be served on all levels and in all those in authority.

I thank You for hearing and answering my prayers, petitions, requests, and supplications. May Your will be done on earth as it is in heaven in the mighty name of Jesus I pray. Amen!

(Reference Scriptures: 2 Chronicles 7:14, Job 12:23-25, Psalms 22:28, Proverbs 11:14, Proverbs 21:1, Proverbs 28:2, Proverbs 29:2, Jeremiah 29:7, Daniel 2:20-23, Matthew 6:10, Mark 11:24, Romans 13:1-14, 1 Timothy 2:1-6, Titus 3:1-2, 1 Peter 2:17)

PRAYERS FOR AGING PARENTS
AND THE ELDERLY

Dear Heavenly Father,

I lift up my aging parents, senior citizens, and the elderly everywhere and ask that You pour out Your mercy and grace on each one. Send forth Your ministering angels to encamp around them providing safety, security, and longevity. Lord, I ask that if any are lost that You would save and deliver them now. Send someone to them that they will listen to and soften their hearts to receive salvation and deliverance.

Protect each one from the enemy of their souls and from evil people that seek to do them any harm or danger. Provide them safety in their frailty and surround them with loving caring people. Lord God, please in Your loving kindness provide each one of them with the spiritual, physical, mental, emotional, and financial support as well as resources and people they need in order to thrive. I pray that You bless each one and especially look after the widows that have no family to care for them.

Lord God please protect their health, food, and water. Protect them whether they are alone or living in a care facility. See to it Lord that their home, or dwelling place are properly maintained.

Lord God I pray that they continually get proper attention and care from all their medical providers, assistants, care takers, case workers, children, family members, church members, and community. Protect and prolong any and all financial investments that sustain them.

Protect each of them from thieves, robbers, and abusers. Give them peace, Your peace that passes all understanding. Remove and protect them from seen and unseen fears and phobias. Guard their minds, be merciful regarding their health and the quality of their health being maintained.

Strengthen their stamina and faith. Increase their joy, and bless their posterity. I thank You for hearing and answering my prayers as I stand in agreement with Your will and the prayers of others interceding for their parents, grandparents, and the elderly population in general.

You're a great, gracious, and loving God! There's no one like You! I pray this prayer in the precious name of Jesus. Amen!

(Reference Scriptures: Psalms 41:3, Psalms 71:1-9, Psalms 103:1-22, Isaiah 40:29, Isaiah 46:4, Mark 11:24, Acts 20:35, Ephesians 6:2-3, 1 Timothy 5:1-4, 8, 16-18, 21-22)

PRAYERS FOR CHILDREN AND GENERATIONS TO COME

Dear Heavenly Father,

I lift up my child/children _____ before You today. I thank You for Your promises of household salvation and deliverance for my lineage. Cause _____ to remember You, our Creator in the days of his/her youth. Place a strong desire in _____ to seek first Your kingdom and Your ways above all else.

Help each of us to consistently speak of Your love and faithfulness in order that none of the coming generations ever forgets You or Your precepts. May we each enjoy Your friendship all the days of our lives. Help us in areas of unbelief and doubt because there is nothing impossible for You Father God.

Strengthen _____ faith and trust in You. Grant each of us repentance, bring us to our senses and deliver us out of any and all snares of the devil. Deliver us in Your loving kindness and tender mercies. Dear Lord where ever I have fallen short as a parent or as a godly example in living holy and walking uprightly before _____, I ask that Your mercy, grace, and forgiveness prevail.

Whatever the enemy has meant for our harm or uses as a tool of distraction from living Your purpose, please turn it around for our good and Your glory. I ask that You not let my sins and shortcomings be placed on _____. Please let my sins remain on me alone.

Forgive me where I have failed as a parent and I ask that You help _____ to honor You and do right by You with his/her own children. Safety comes from You Lord God so protect _____ from the enemy of his/her soul. Grant long life to _____ .

Help _____ to honor his/her parents. Keep me from provoking _____ to wrath leading him/her to sin, rebellion, and away from You. Send forth Your ministering angels to encamp around _____ and keep seen and unseen evil, evil people, ungodly intentions that come from peer pressure, and potential dangers far away from him/her.

I thank You for showing Yourself mighty to _____ . May he/she have true fellowship with You all the days of his/her life. I bless _____ in the name of the Lord Jesus Christ. Bless and protect his/her mind and health. Fend off chemical imbalances, sicknesses, diseases, worries, depression, oppression, wrong-thinking, and ungodly desires.

Increase Your presence in _____ life. Give wisdom, understanding, knowledge, and strong discernment in his/her decision making, free-will, and choices. Intervene, intercept, and interfere when needed. Provide Your Divine interception and order _____ steps for him/her to fulfill Your purpose, call, and plans in his/her life.

Please create great stewardship in him/her. Teach_____ to consistently order his/her days and time. Help him/her to count the cost before making choices and decisions. Keep _____ humble and honest. Teach him/her to protect and maintain his/her integrity and walk uprightly before You all the days of his/her life.

I ask that You put up Your standard against the lures of this world. Lord please prevent the cares of this world, the deceitfulness of riches, and the desire for other things that come to choke out Your Word or delay Your purpose for _____ life. Let Your will be done on earth as it is in heaven. Teach and give great understanding to _____ in the area of giving and receiving.

Help him/her to manage money and all financial matters wisely. Give _____ a desire to work, live a quiet and peaceable life. Quickly expose and eliminate all attitudes of selfishness, entitlement, pride, greed, lust, and self-reliance. Help him/her to love You genuinely, fear You and obey Your boundaries. I ask the Holy Spirit to help _____ walk in the love of God that has been shed abroad in his/her heart. I ask that You sanctify _____ with Your truth and give him/her a desire, thirst, and hunger for Your Word and for living a life worthy of the call You have on his/her life.

Surround _____ with all godly influences whether through friends, family members, professionals, school teachers, professors, co-workers, and bosses. May he/she be a dependable witness for You. May _____ come to know You personally. Allow Your influence to always be present in his/her life. I rejoice always in Your love for us.

Thank You Father God for hearing, answering prayers and supplications concerning my child/children and for our future generations. I trust You to work out all things concerning _____ regardless of present circumstances. I stand in faith believing that You will work out all things.

It's in the mighty name of Jesus I pray. Amen!

(Reference Scriptures: Psalms 26:1-12, Psalms 71:17-18, Psalms 78:1-7, Psalms 90:12, Psalms 112:1-9, Psalms 113:7-9, Psalms 115:13-16, Psalms 116:1-2, Psalms 117:1-2, Psalms 118:1-9, Proverbs 13:24, Proverbs 15:33, Proverbs 20:20, Proverbs 22:6, Proverbs 29:15 and 17, Proverbs 30:17, Ecclesiastes 12:1, 13-14, Jeremiah 29:11, Matthew 6:10, Matthew 15:1-20, Mark 4:14-20, Mark 11:24, Acts 2:38-39, Acts 16:31, Ephesians 6:1-4, Philippians 4:6)

PRAYERS FOR SPOUSES

Dear Heavenly Father,

I lift up my husband/wife _____ before You today. I thank You for Your promises of household salvation and deliverance. Lord God, I ask that You please bless our relationship in ways we never considered. Bless our union and marriage. May we be a great example to others for Your glory. Help us to pray together more often and stand in agreement with Your Word at all times.

Help us both to be great listeners towards each other and help us to hear You clearly in all things. Please expose and remove any divisiveness or division that has or may try to come in between us. Keep us from nagging, complaining, and murmuring about each other's flaws and shortcomings.

Shut down any and all distractions that would try to come in and tear our relationship apart. Help us both to have a healthy family unit. Where I am weak, I thank You for _____ strength. Remind us both to be subject to each other. Keep us both from allowing any bitterness or resentment to lie undetected and unforgiven.

Reveal and restore any areas of unforgiveness. When needed, please grant each of us repentance, bring us to our senses, and deliver us out of the snares of the devil.

Thank You for Your grace and tender mercies everyday. Give my husband/wife _____ a heart for You and a strong desire to walk before You uprightly all the days of his/her life. Help me to love _____ the way You love me. Holy Spirit help me to walk in the love of God towards _____ that has been shed abroad in my heart. Lord please bless _____ on his/her job, bless and prosper him/her.

Surround him/her with Your favor. Please help him/her to be prepared for the opportunities that are ahead of him/her that You want _____ to partake of in the future. Lord God You know _____ desires and prayers that are before You. I ask that Your will be done concerning those things he/she has before You. Lord Your Word says that You delight in the prosperity of Your servants. God please prosper _____ soul, health, relationships, finances, and increase the fellowship he/she has with You.

Safety comes from You Lord God, please protect and keep _____ from harm, evil people, and all plans of the enemy. Send forth Your ministering angels to work Your plans out for him/her and keep him/her safe at all times. Please provide traveling mercies for _____. Give him/her Your peace. Please increase Your wisdom, knowledge, understanding, and discernment in him/her. Protect _____ mind and body.

Lord help him/her overcome any ungodly fears, misunderstandings, worries, or apprehensions that would prevent his/her growth in You. Help any areas of doubt and unbelief. Show Yourself mighty and victorious to _____ because nothing is impossible with You Lord God.

Please increase _____ faith and trust in You today in the ways that You know gets his/her attention. I thank You Lord for hearing my prayers, requests, and supplications concerning _____ and our relationship. I praise You for answering these prayers for my husband/wife and for strengthening our marriage. Thank You Lord! It's in the precious name of Your son, Jesus Christ I pray these prayers for my husband/wife and our marriage. Amen!

(Reference Scriptures: Genesis 1:27-28, Genesis 2:18-24, Joshua 1:9, Proverbs 3:5-6, Ecclesiastes 4:12, Ecclesiastes 9:9, Isaiah 54:5, Jeremiah 23:11, Matthew 6:8-15, Matthew 6:25-34, Matthew 19:1-12, Mark 10:9, Mark 11:24, Acts 16:31, Romans 8:28, 1 Corinthians 7:1-16, 1 Corinthians 10:13, Ephesians 2:8-9, Ephesians 4:2-3, Ephesians 4:32, Ephesians 5:1 Ephesians 5:22-33, Hebrews 13:4, 1 Peter 4:8, 1 John 4:7-8)

PRAYERS FOR SHUT-IN
AND DISABLED PERSONS

Dear Heavenly Father,

You know the people who are disabled and some are shut-in due to mental and/or physical handicaps that need You and Your provisions in a special way today. I ask that You please minister to each one today and look out for them in a mighty way. Some have no one standing in the gap interceding for them, but today You have raised me up to pray for others around the world who need Your salvation, deliverance, and special attention.

Please send forth Your mighty angels to defend the helpless, disabled, and shut-in today around the world. Nothing is to big or impossible for You Lord God. You know everything and everyone on this planet. You keep count of every hair on our heads and You know our days. Your Word says You knew each one of us before we were fashioned and made in our mother's womb.

I know You hear my prayers and Your Word never returns void. You've called Your children to pray and intercede for the lost, the poor, and for others in need. I lift up the shut-in and disable today to You the all powerful, all knowing, and loving God. Your mercy endures forever. Lord please meet every need and send the provisions, care, people, supplies, support, and resources today to those who cannot fend for themselves, relying on the physical help of someone else. I lift up the caretakers today as well. Give the caretakers peace, patience, stamina, and love for those that need their strength, might, and services in any capacity.

Please restore those caretakers and rejuvenate them right now Lord God. I ask that You protect the disabled and shut in from evil, wicked people, thieves, and the enemy of their souls. Thank You for hearing and answering my prayers. Help and position me to be a blessing to those in need wherever they may be, and in whatever capacity You deem fit for me to assist.

Thank You for giving me a voice to stand in the gap interceding for those with special needs today. It's in the mighty name of Jesus I pray these requests. Amen!

(Reference Scriptures: Leviticus 19:14, Exodus 4:11, 2 Samuel Chapter 9, Psalms 103:13-14, Psalms 103:20-22, Psalms 139:13-14, Psalms 145:9, Isaiah 1:17, Matthew 5:5, Matthew 18:4-5 and verse 10, Mark 11:24, Luke 14:12-13, John 9:2-7, Romans 5:3-5, 2 Corinthians 12:7-10, Ephesians 2:10, Hebrews 13:1-3, James 1:27, James 5:11)

PRAYERS FOR MILITARY PERSONNEL

Dear Heavenly Father,

I lift up prayers and intercession for our military soldiers, men and women of valor, the leaders of each branch, and all those in command. Give Your guidance, wisdom, understanding, knowledge, discernment, and great counsel to all those making tactical to strategic decisions that will affect the lives of each individual in any capacity of our military service personnel as well as all civilians involved. Please provide that same guidance and counsel concerning those in harms way and in the line of fire.

God please help and assist those that are assigned to follow difficult missions and pursuits. I ask that You place a hedge of protection around each man and woman serving. Send forth Your ministering angels to uphold Your safety and protection during battles and those stationed on foreign soil. Increase allies, support, and resources needed ahead of time. Provide the best equipment and materials needed to assist those in service.

If there are any that do not know You, please send someone that they will listen to in order to receive their salvation. Dear Lord, I ask that You protect their minds, souls, and bodies. You know and understand the affect wars and battles have on individuals and countries. Please create preparation and provisions for all Your saints everywhere. I pray that Your will be done on earth as it is in heaven concerning these matters.

Strengthen and encourage each one serving away from home.

Provide comfort and peace for each of their family members. Pour out Your wisdom, understanding, knowledge, blessings, support, resources, and assistance for all the fathers, mothers, grandparents, siblings, husbands, wives, and children and all those that have family members and loved ones serving in our military.

Please keep the spouses of those serving in the military protected and loyal. Heal sadness and broken heartedness. Lord God, please provide emotional support, greater financial provisions, and spiritual healing to all those in service as well as those returning home. Please strengthen and heal the mental health of our soldiers returning from the battles fought. Help each of them to deescalate safely and as quickly as possible from traumatic stressors suffered from war. Lord please help each one return back into society peaceably and honorably.

Help their transferable skills be easily recognizable by potential employers for those returning to the work force. Please minister greatly to those that have suffered any kind of loss physically. Help each one to get the best medical care available as long as needed. Pour out Your favor and great grace as they return to their families. Please provide great grace for all Veterans. Thank You! I give You all the praise, all the glory for hearing and answering my prayers, supplications, and requests in the mighty name of Jesus I pray. Amen!

(Reference Scriptures: Deuteronomy 20:1-4, Psalms 4:8, Psalms 5:8, Psalms 23:4-6, Psalms 24:8, Psalms 27:1, Psalms 40:14, Psalms 46:1, Psalms 55:22, Psalms 91:1-16, Psalms 103:20-22, Psalms 108:12-13, Psalms 138:3, Psalms 138:7-8, Psalms 144:1-2, Psalms 147:3, Proverbs 4:7, Proverbs 21:31,

Ecclesiastes 3:8, Isaiah 26:3, Isaiah 54:17, Joel 2:32, Nahum 1:7, Matthew 6:10, Matthew 11:28, Matthew 19:26, Mark 11:24, John 3:16, John 15:13, Ephesians 6:10-18, Philippians 4:13, 2 Timothy 1:7, James 1:5)

PRAYERS FOR LAW ENFORCEMENT OFFICERS

Dear Heavenly Father,

I lift up all those that are in command as well as in charge of protecting citizens, civilians, and enforcing the laws of the land today. Father God You understand and know all things especially justice and injustices. You understand and know the dangers involved when the laws are being enforced in any capacity. You know and understand the preciseness needed when it comes to making a judgment call in every situation involving seen or unseen dangers.

You also know and understand the frailty of humans because You created all people. You know the motives and intentions of the hearts of all people. You know errors that men and women make before any situations ever take place. Therefore, I pray that You send forth Your ministering angels to protect and serve those that abide by the laws, enforce the laws, and administer the laws. Bring those that practice lawlessness to justice and Your justice.

Give strong wisdom, keen insight, total understanding, and great discernment to the law enforcement officers that are serving the citizens of this country today. Help these officers supernaturally to discern real danger and evil pretenses so they can act accordingly. Equip them with preparedness. Protect their lives on every front. Help their minds to remain sharp and judgments to be right. Heal emotional traumas and subside outside stressors that would work to erode or destroy these officers in their personal lives.

Protect the families of each officer. Comfort the hearts of the parents, siblings, spouses, and children of each officer.

Bless the men and women who work in any capacity of law enforcement today. Save any that are lost, needing You as their Lord and Savior. Be gracious unto those that work in harms way everyday.

Please bless their families, personal health, minds, spirits, and finances as they work for their pay and serve the public.

Thank You for showing Your loving kindness, forgiveness, grace, mercy, protection, and provisions for each one in the law enforcement field today. Thank You for the good that they strive to accomplish. Strengthen and expand the good intentions, the good will.

Remove evil and wrong intentions all together. I pray that Your will be done on earth as it is in heaven concerning these prayers, supplications, and requests made on all law enforcements behalf today.

Thank You for hearing and answering these prayers in the mighty name of Jesus I pray. Amen!

(Reference Scriptures: Psalms 27:1, Psalms 40:14, Psalms 91:1-16, Psalms 103:20-22, Psalms 138:3, Psalms 138:7-8, Psalms 147:3, Proverbs 4:7, Proverbs 21:31, Matthew 6:10, Matthew 11:28, Matthew 19:26, Mark 11:24, John 15:13, Romans 13:1-5, Philippians 4:13, 1 Timothy 2:1-3, 2 Timothy 1:7, Titus 3:1, James 1:5, 1 Peter 2:13-14, 1 Peter 5:5)

PRAYERS FOR FIRE FIGHTERS
AND EMERGENCY RESPONDERS

Dear Heavenly Father,

I lift up every Fire Fighter and Emergency Responder that works to protect civilians today. Please protect their lives as they place them in harms way to save others in any situation that occurs. Give them great wisdom, understanding, and discernment in all areas. Strengthen their minds and bodies to be quick and accurate.

When attempting rescue missions or operations, please give them the wisdom and insight needed to survive as well as save others they are sent to help. Let the Holy Spirit guide them. Safety comes from You Lord God. I pray that You send forth Your mighty and ministering angels to protect as well as assist these going into dangerous situations today. I pray that You save any that are lost and need Jesus Christ, Your son as their Lord and Savior.

I lift up the families related to each Fire Fighter and Emergency Responder. Please provide Your peace of mind and comfort the hearts of the parents, siblings, spouses, and children of those that work these types of jobs in any capacity. Show Your wonderful grace and mercy in all ways.

Provide the provisions necessary to sustain their lives on and off the job. Remove fears and provide tactical insight in dangerous or perilous matters. Help them to see what others cannot see and rely on You and Your power saving techniques.

Thank You so much for every one of them that work these types of jobs protecting and pulling us out of harms way when needed.

I pray that You personally look out for them and their needs at all times. I thank You, I praise You for hearing these prayers, supplications, and requests for all Fire Fighters and Emergency Responders every where that work to save others. Bless and keep these men and women in the mighty name of Jesus. Amen!

(Reference Scriptures: Psalms 91:1-16, Psalms 103:20-22, Psalms 138:3, Psalms 138:7-8, Proverbs 4:7, Proverbs 21:31, Matthew 6:10, Matthew 19:26, Mark 11:24, John 15:13, Philippians 4:13, 2 Timothy 1:7)

PRAYERS FOR SCHOOLS, STUDENTS, TEACHERS AND EDUCATORS

Dear Heavenly Father,

I lift up every school, teacher, and educator today. I pray that You protect all the students from pre-school age all the way to college. Please protect the schools, college campuses, teachers, and educators as well as those who serve or work with our children in every capacity.

Lord, safety comes from You. Please send forth Your ministering angels to protect and help our children, schools, colleges, teachers, educators, and all employees that work in this field.

Expose and remove any evil plots affecting students across this country today. Please keep and bless those that are not able to defend themselves. Save the lost and deliver those in dire situations. Please send the help, funds, people, volunteers, resources, supplies, tools, and materials needed for all teachers, assistants, educators, and students.

I pray that You pour out Your wisdom, understanding, knowledge, and academic progression for all our students. Put a desire in each child to love learning and make the teachers' job joyous while removing the burdens of bureaucracy. May Your truth prevail over all.

Pour out Your Spirit of excellence on each student. Give an attitude of obedience in our children towards authority figures, increase better behavior more and more from the youngest to the oldest. Improve the people, functionality, materials, processes, and systems that are set in place in order to create as well as facilitate growth, knowledge, and expertise.

Please provide innovative technologies that enhance the teaching and learning experiences. Increase the respect towards the profession over all. Provide witty inventions and creative ideas that will increase the income of those that teach, educate, and empower our children now.

Please protect the health and spirit of each child. Remove all inefficiencies, ill-will, evil, and ungodliness towards the children, students, schools, teachers, and educators.

Bless and increase those that uphold Your standards in every area. Protect and bless their families. Guard the hearts of the next generation. Have Your way across this land. May Your will be done on earth as it is in heaven concerning these matters and prayers.

Thank You Lord for hearing my prayers and I give You all the praise for answering these prayers today in the mighty name of Jesus. Amen!

(Reference Scriptures: Psalms 103:20-22, Proverbs 4:7, Proverbs 4:13, Proverbs 15:5, Proverbs 16:9, Proverbs 22:6, Matthew 6:10, Matthew 10:24, Mark 12:17, Luke 6:40, Romans 13:1-5, 1 Corinthians 15:58, Ephesians 6:1-3, Colossians 3:16, Colossians 3:20, 1 Timothy 2:1-3, 2 Timothy 2:15, Titus 2:3-5, Titus 2:7-8, Titus 3:1, Hebrews 13:17, James 1:5, James 3:1-2, 1 Peter 2:13-14, 1 Peter 3:15, 1 Peter 5:5)

PRAYER FOR GOD'S LOVE TO SHOW

Dear Heavenly Father,

I pray that You please help me to show Your love through my words and actions. Your Word says that love covers a multitude of sins and without demonstrating love I am nothing.

Lord God, I want to please You and sincerely demonstrate the love of Christ Jesus to all. I want to obey Your principles Lord. Holy Spirit, please help me to love others with the love of God that has been shed abroad in my heart in the mighty name of Jesus I pray. Thank You Lord God!   Amen!

(Reference Scriptures: Matthew 5:43-48, Matthew 22:36-40, Luke 6:27-36, Mark 11:24, Mark 12:30-31, Romans 5:5-8, Romans 13:8-10, 1 Corinthians 13, 1 Peter 4:8, 1 John 5:1-3)

PRAYER TO ABOUND IN THE DIVINE NATURE

Dear Heavenly Father,

According to Your Word and by Your divine power You have given me everything that I need to live a godly life. You have given me great and precious promises enabling me to share in Your divine nature escaping the world's corruption caused by human desire. Therefore, Lord God thank You for helping me to make every effort to respond accurately to Your promises. Thank You for helping me to increase and abound in the fruits of Your divine nature.

I will be diligent to add to my faith, virtue/moral excellence, to moral excellence knowledge, to knowledge self-control, to self-control perseverance, to perseverance godliness, to godliness brotherly kindness, and to brotherly kindness love. Please increase my desire to want to know Jesus Christ more and more everyday while abounding in these so I will be neither barren nor unfruitful in the knowledge of the Lord Jesus Christ. Thank You for giving me a mindset and a spirit of diligence in order for me to make my call and election sure by doing these things so that I will never stumble!

In the mighty name of Jesus I pray to abound in Your divine nature all the days of my life. Amen!

(Reference Scriptures: Mark 11:24, 2 Peter 1:1-10)

PRAYER TO OVERCOME FEAR

Dear Heavenly Father,

I repent for entertaining the thoughts of fears that are lies about myself, others, and situations in or out of my control in the name of Jesus I pray. God, Your Word says that I am to trust You completely because You did not give me a spirit of fear, but have given me power, a sound mind, and love.

Heavenly Father, I renounce all agreements with any panics, anxieties, worries, and anxious thoughts that I have been ensnared with concerning my life and in the matter of

_____ .

Your Word instructs me not to fear anything except You because You are with me wherever I go. I choose to trust You. You are my God, my refuge, my strength, and my confidence is in You and Your promises of protection and provision. I choose to stand in faith and watch Your salvation come to pass concerning _____ . Thank You Lord God for Your mighty hand of deliverance in Jesus name I pray. Amen!

(Reference Scriptures: Psalms 27:1, Psalms 34:4, Psalms Chapter 46, Psalms 55:22, Psalms Chapter 145, Psalms 147:11, Proverbs 3:5-8, Proverbs 29:25, Isaiah 41:10, Jeremiah 32:17, Matthew 6:25-34, Matthew 10:28, Luke 12:4-6, Romans 8:26-28, Romans 8:37-39, Philippians 1:6, Philippians 4:6-7, Philippians 4:13, 2 Timothy 1:7, 1 Peter 5:6-7, Jude 1:24-25)

PRAYER TO GUARD FROM DECEPTION

Dear Heavenly Father,

I ask that You please break off any deceptions that have crept into my mind, will, emotions, and soul. Protect me from choosing to believe what I want to believe over what I should believe whether there is evidence or not. Remove me from choosing willful unbelief concerning the truth in all matters. When I know what is right, when I know Your commandments, help me to choose to obey rather than choosing to disobey and reject You dear Heavenly Father.

Please reveal quickly any of my own evil desires that are lurking within me that want self satisfaction over knowing and obeying Your truth. Keep me from liking wrongdoing. Please don't allow me to resist You. Help me to bridle my tongue. Protect me in areas that I may be naïve and gullible towards deception. Restore integrity within me.

Lord God I implore You by Your tender mercies to please guard and deliver me from the grip of deception and self deception. Shine Your light and truth on my mind and give me wisdom and discernment. Renew my mind completely and line my mind up with Your Word in the name of Jesus I pray! Amen!

(Reference Scriptures: Deuteronomy 11:16, Job 15:31, Psalms 101:4-5, Proverbs 11:13, Proverbs 20:1, Proverbs 20:19, Matthew 7:21-23, Matthew 13:22, John 12:37, Romans 12:2, 1 Corinthians 6:9-10, 1 Corinthians 15:33, Galatians 6:7-8, Ephesians 5:6, Colossians 2:8, 2 Thessalonians 2:9-11, 1 Timothy 5:13, 2 Timothy 3:13-14, James 1:5, James 1:14-16,

James 1:21-26, James 4:17, 2 Peter 3:9, 1 John 1:8, 1 John 4:1, 1 John 2:15-17)

PRAYER TO SHARPEN
THE SWORD OF THE SPIRIT

Dear Heavenly Father,

According to Your Word in Ephesians 3:20, it says that You are able to do exceedingly abundantly above all that we ask or think, according to the power that works in us. Lord God, Your Word is powerful. I desire to use Your Word to overcome the enemy. I want to know how to use Your Word effectively and accurately in every area of my life. I choose to be teachable Lord.

As I hear Your Word preached or spoken as well as when I personally read, study, meditate, or memorize Your Word in any capacity, I ask and pray that You sharpen the sword of the Spirit in me so Your power will be mightier in me in the name of Jesus I pray. Thank You Lord God! Amen!

(Reference Scriptures: Matthew 4:4, Mark 11:24, Ephesians 3:20-21, Ephesians 6:17, Ephesians 6:10-18, , 2 Corinthians 10:3-6, 2 Timothy 2:15, 2 Timothy 3:16-17, Hebrews 1:3, Hebrews 4:12, Luke 11:28, James 1:21, Joshua 1:8, Psalms 18:30, Psalms 119:9, Psalms 119:11, Psalms 119:33-40, Psalms 119:99-105)

CHAPTER ONE

SPIRITUAL
DECREES, DECLARES & PRAYERS

**The tongue has the power
of life and death.**

Proverbs 18:21

**Thou shalt also decree a thing, and it
shall be established unto thee: and
the light shall shine upon thy ways.**

Job 22:28

**I decree, declare, and pray that every
good and perfect gift comes down from
the Father of light; therefore, today shall
end good and it shall end perfect
in Jesus' name I pray!**

James 1:17

We are created in the image and likeness of God. Therefore, **our words** will not return void to us either. (Reference Scriptures: Genesis 1:26-27, Isaiah 55:10-11, Matthew 12:33-37)

I decree, declare, and pray that every good and perfect gift comes down from above from God the Father of lights. Therefore, this day shall end good and it shall end perfect in the name of Jesus I pray. (Reference Scripture: James 1:17)

I decree, declare, and pray that I have a hope for my future, therefore, I have power in my present day as I choose to speak of the wonderful works of God in the name of Jesus I pray. (Reference Scriptures: Psalms 30:5, Jeremiah 23:11, Habakkuk 2:3, Acts 2:11)

I decree, declare, and pray that I choose to yield to the Holy Spirit. I yield the members of my body to the Holy Spirit so the Holy Spirit will grow bigger and stronger in my life in the name of Jesus I pray. (Reference Scriptures: John 16:12-15, Romans 8:26, Romans 12:1-2, 1 Corinthians 6:19-20, 2 Corinthians 10:3, Galatians 5:25, Philippians 1:19-21, Ephesians 3:16, Philippians 4:13)

I decree, declare, and pray that I have a thirst for doing things God's way in the name of Jesus I pray. (Reference Scriptures: Isaiah 44:3, John 4:14)

I decree, declare, and pray that Christ is living inside me the hope of glory dwells inside me. Therefore, all things are possible with God for me in the name of Jesus I pray. (Reference Scriptures: Luke 1:37, 2 Corinthians 6:16, Colossians 1:27, 1 John 4:4)

I decree, declare, and pray that I walk by faith and not by the sight of my circumstances in the name of Jesus I pray. (Reference Scriptures: 2 Corinthians 5:7, Hebrews 11:1, Hebrews 11:6)

I decree, declare, and pray that my latter days will be greater than my former days. I am blessed and favored of the Lord in the name of Jesus I pray. (Reference Scriptures: 1 Samuel 2: 9-10, Haggai 2:7-9, Psalms 5:12, Psalms 18:35, Psalms 35:1, Psalms 84:11, Psalms 118:15, Proverbs 20:22, Romans 8:28, 1 Corinthians 15:57, 2 Corinthians 2:14, 2 Corinthians 4:7)

I decree, declare, and pray there is power in the name of Jesus. There is power in the blood of Jesus. Every demonic influence and evil power must bow and go when I speak the name of Jesus and by the blood of Jesus Christ. In the mighty name of Jesus I pray. (Reference Scriptures: Proverbs 18:10, Isaiah 9:6, Jeremiah 10:6, Malachi 1:11, Matthew 1:21, Matthew 28:18, Mark 16:17, Luke 10:17-23, John 14:13, John 16:33, Acts 4:12, Romans 1:20, Colossians 1:12-20, Philippians 2:9-11, Revelation 12:11)

I decree, declare, and pray that my gift makes room for me and I use the gift accurately that God has given me in the name of Jesus I pray. (Reference Scripture: Proverbs 18:16)

I decree, declare, and pray that I love and pursue all the ordinances of the Lord God in the name of Jesus I pray. (Reference Scripture: Psalms 19:9)

I decree, declare, and pray that willful sins do not rule me, I am under God's grace, and I choose to walk in the fruit of the Holy Spirit in all my ways in the name of Jesus I pray. (Reference Scriptures: Psalms 19:13, Romans 6:14, Galatians 5:16)

I decree, declare, and pray that I keep short accounts with God. I do not let sins accumulate in my life in the name of Jesus I pray. (Reference Scripture: 1 John 1:9)

I decree, declare, and pray that the Lord God is my Rock and redeemer I am steadfast in the faith walking in love, trusting God through my trials and tribulations in the name of Jesus I pray. (Reference Scriptures: Psalms 18:2, Psalms 91:1-16, 1 Corinthians 15:58, 2 Thessalonians 3:5, 1 Peter 5:8-9,2 Peter 3:17, James 1:2-4)

I decree, declare, and pray that I love learning from God's Word and I follow His Words in the name of Jesus I pray. (Reference Scriptures: Deuteronomy 6:5, Matthew 22:37, Luke 10:26-28)

I decree, declare, and pray that the Holy Spirit spares me from self imposed hardships and when problems do come I can face them with calmness and a confident attitude because I am aware of God's resources that enable me to deal with adversity in the name of Jesus I pray. (Reference Scriptures: Proverbs 16:3, 2 Corinthians 10:3-7, Galatians 5:16-26, Ephesians 6:10-18, Philippians 4:12-13, James 4:7)

I decree, declare, and pray that when I have had enough in life with feelings of not going on whether from feelings of disappointments, fears, failures, weariness, or grudges; I automatically run to God who is the only one that can help me. I choose to seek Him with my whole heart. God really loves me, understands me, and is truly the lifter of my head in the name of Jesus I pray. (Reference Scriptures: 1 Chronicles 28:9, Psalms 3:3, Psalms 86:15, Jeremiah 29:13, Hosea 10:12, Zephaniah 3:17, Psalms 14:2, Romans 5:8, Romans 8:37-39, Galatians 2:20, Hebrews 11:6, James 1:2-4)

I decree, declare, and pray that I communicate with God personally through listening to God speak, reading and meditating on His scriptures and praying daily in the name of Jesus I pray. (Reference Scriptures: 2 Timothy 3:16-17, Psalms 4:1)

I decree, declare, and pray that God's Word has equipped me for every good work in the name of Jesus I pray. (Reference Scriptures: 2 Timothy 3:16-17)

I decree, declare, and pray that I hold firmly to the faith in God I profess, fighting the good fight of faith victoriously in the name of Jesus I pray. (Reference Scriptures: 1 Corinthians 15:57, 1 Timothy 6:12, Hebrews 4:13-14)

I decree, declare, and pray that I am diligent to the very end making my hope sure. I am aiming to hear God say to me, well done, good and faithful servant. In the name of Jesus I pray. (Reference Scriptures: Matthew 25:21, Hebrews 6:11)

I decree, declare, and pray that I lean not on my own understanding, in all my ways I acknowledge the Lord and He directs my paths in the name of Jesus I pray. (Reference Scriptures: Psalms 3:5-6, Proverbs 3:5-6)

I decree, declare, and pray that I am refusing to link failures to my self esteem because failures are stepping stones to success in the name of Jesus I pray. (Reference Scriptures: Psalms 139:13-14, Proverbs 23:7, Luke 12:7)

I decree, declare, and pray that I am refusing to link failures to my self worth. I am worthy, I am valuable, and I am great because greater is He that is in me than He that is in the world in the name of Jesus I pray. (Reference Scriptures: Psalms 139:13-14, Proverbs 23:7, Luke 12:7, Philippians 1:6, 1 Peter 2:9-10, 1 John 4:4)

I decree, declare, and pray that I believe God is in control and has my best interests at heart. Therefore, I am fully able to trust and obey Him in the name of Jesus I pray. (Reference Scriptures: Psalms 118:6-9, Proverbs 19:21, Jeremiah 29:11, Nahum 1:7, Romans 8:28)

I decree, declare, and pray that I have strong and lasting faith in God in all situations in the name of Jesus I pray. (Reference Scriptures: Joshua 1:9, Hebrews 11:6, Matthew 17:20)

I decree, declare, and pray that I love who I am, who God has created me to be, and I live authentically every day in the name of Jesus I pray. (Reference Scriptures: Romans 13:8, Mark 12:30-31)

I decree, declare, and pray that I am redeemed of the Lord. The Lord has redeemed me from the hand of the enemy. Therefore, I will continually praise Him in the name of Jesus I pray. (Reference Scripture: Psalms 107:2)

I decree, declare, and pray that I always honor the Lord in all that I do and say in the name of Jesus I pray. (Reference Scripture: Colossians 3:17)

I decree, declare, and pray that through Christ Jesus strength I can do all things. In the name of Jesus I pray. (Reference Scripture: Philippians 4:13)

I decree, declare, and pray that I love discipline and knowledge. My behavior and actions line up with the will of God in the name of Jesus I pray. (Reference Scripture: Proverbs 12:1)

I decree, declare, and pray that I am fully aware and fully integrated to what God has called me to do and I apply it daily in the name of Jesus I pray. (Reference Scriptures: Psalms 139, Philippians 1:6)

I decree, declare, and pray that I am fully aware and awake to my potential. I fully embrace each and every aspect of my identity. I know I belong to God and He has my back in all situations in the name of Jesus I pray. (Reference Scriptures: Isaiah 42:16, Isaiah 58:8, Luke 3:5-6, 2 Corinthians 5:17, 1 John 4:4, 1 Peter 2:9)

I decree, declare, and pray that I overcome everything I face by the blood of the Lamb and by the words of my testimony in Jesus name I pray. (Reference Scripture: Revelation 12:11)

I decree, declare, and pray that I know how to see, I have self awareness, I am fully aware of my potential and what is possible in the world around me because God brings me the opportunities to increase for His glory and my good. In the name of Jesus I pray. (Reference Scriptures: 1 Peter 2:9, Galatians 2:20)

I decree, declare, and pray that I always see the possibilities in myself and my God given potential. I can truly see the best in myself and others because God increases my spiritual discernment daily as I walk with Him in the name of Jesus I pray. (Reference Scriptures: Matthew 19:26, Philippians 2:1-11)

I decree, declare, and pray that I know how to align my actions to my desired outcomes and objectives. God increases my steadfastness to effectively produce results and I follow through consistently in the name of Jesus I pray. (Reference Scripture: Proverbs 22:29)

I decree, declare, and pray that God has fully equipped me and I am able to stand against the wiles, tricks, and schemes of the devil because no weapon formed against me shall prosper and every tongue that rises up against me in judgment shall be condemn in the name of Jesus I pray. (Reference Scriptures: Isaiah 54:17, Matthew 16:23, 2 Corinthians 2:10-11, Jude 1:9, Ephesians 6:10-18, James 4:7, 1 John 2:16, 1 John 4:1)

I decree, declare, and pray that I fully understand and exercise daily the power and authority I have in Jesus Christ in the name of Jesus I pray. (Reference Scriptures: Ephesians 2:10, Matthew 28:18-20, 2 Timothy 1:7)

I decree, declare, and pray that I have mastery over my fleshly desires, thoughts, words, and deeds. I am humble, I am disciplined. I cast down every imagination and thought that exalts itself against the knowledge of God bringing every thought into the captivity to the obedience of Christ because I have the mind of Christ Jesus and I choose to walk in the Spirit consistently in the name of Jesus I pray. (Reference Scriptures: Psalms 19:14, 1 Corinthians 2:16, 2 Corinthians 5:20-21, 2 Corinthians 10:2-6, Galatians 5:16, 2 Timothy 1:7 Amplified Bible Version, James 2:24, James Chapter 2, James Chapter 3, James 4:1-12)

I decree, declare, and pray that I submit myself to the Lord and resist the devil, temptations, and choices that delay my progress for spiritual maturity, growth, and improvement in the name of Jesus I pray. (Reference Scriptures: 2 Timothy 1:7 Amplified Bible Version, James 4:7-10)

I decree, declare, and pray that I delight myself in the Lord in the name of Jesus I pray. (Reference Scriptures: Psalms 37:4, Psalms 63:1 & 6)

I decree, declare, and pray that I always deal with anger, bitterness, and fear God's way by putting into practice forgiveness and speaking what is written in the Word of God in the name of Jesus I pray. God is my true healer, Savior, provider, and deliverer. No weapon formed against me shall prosper in the name of Jesus I pray. (Reference Scriptures: Isaiah 54:17, Ephesians 4:31-32, Ephesians Chapter 4 in The Message Bible Version, 2 Timothy 1:7)

I decree, declare, and pray that I am forgiven, released from all fear, shame, unbelief, and guilt from all my former sins. I am open to the Holy Spirit to speak His truth to me and heal my heart, mind, emotions, and body in the name of Jesus I pray. (Reference Scriptures: John 3:14-21, John 16:13, John 14:26)

I decree, declare, and pray that I have strong faith in God standing firm and courageous in all situations because I have the victory that is in Christ Jesus in the name of Jesus I pray. (Reference Scriptures: 1 Corinthians 16:13-14)

I decree, declare, and pray that I commit my ways to the Lord and trust Him completely in the name of Jesus I pray. (Reference Scripture: Psalms 37:5)

I decree, declare, and pray that I am still before the Lord and wait patiently for Him in the name of Jesus I pray. (Reference Scripture: Psalms 37:7)

I decree, declare, and pray that I refrain from anger and turn from wrath in the name of Jesus I pray.
(Reference Scripture: Psalms 37:8)

I decree, declare, and pray that I always place my hope in the Lord in the name of Jesus I pray.
(Reference Scripture: Psalms 37:9)

I decree, declare, and pray that I am meek; I am calm in my responses in the name of Jesus I pray.
(Reference Scripture: Psalms 37:11)

I decree, declare, and pray that I have funds and resources to do whatever needs to be done or paid for at the moment needed, so that I can lend generously and freely in the name of Jesus I pray.
(Reference Scriptures: Psalms 37:25-26, Luke 6:38, Philippians 4:19)

I decree, declare, and pray that I seek and love wisdom. My mouth utters wisdom and my tongue speaks what is just in the name of Jesus I pray.
(Reference Scripture: Psalms 37:30)

I decree, declare, and pray that the laws and understanding of God's principles are in my heart in the name of Jesus I pray. (Reference Scripture: Psalms 37:31)

I decree, declare, and pray that I wait patiently for the Lord and keep His ways in the name of Jesus I pray. (Reference Scripture: Psalms 37:34)

I decree, declare, and pray that I consider the blameless, observe the upright and I am a person of peace in the name of Jesus I pray. (Reference Scripture: Psalms 37:37)

I decree, declare, and pray that I take refuge in the Lord. The Lord always helps, delivers, and saves me from the wicked in the name of Jesus I pray. (Reference Scriptures: Psalms 37:40, Psalms 91)

I decree, declare, and pray that I put up resistance against procrastination. I am productive and I get my work done on time in the name of Jesus I pray. (Reference Scriptures: Ecclesiastes 11:4, Proverbs 18:9)

I decree, declare, and pray that my brain chemistry functions properly and I have the victory over depression. I am more than a conqueror through Christ Jesus in the name of Jesus I pray. (Reference Scripture: Psalms 147:3, Romans 8:35-39)

I decree, declare, and pray that I have the love of God in me. I choose to demonstrate love towards others and I practice showing love towards my enemies in the name of Jesus I pray. (Reference Scriptures: Matthew 5:43-48, Romans 5:5, 1 Corinthians 13:1-13)

I decree, declare, and pray that I operate in power, sound mind, mental clarity, and love in the name of Jesus I pray. (Reference Scriptures: 1 Corinthians 2:9-10 and 12-16, 2 Timothy 1:7)

I decree, declare, and pray that I strongly desire spiritual gifts so I can share them with others in the name of Jesus I pray. (Reference Scripture: 1 Corinthians 14:1)

I decree, declare, and pray that I consistently lift others up for their strengthening, encouragement, comfort, and edification in the name of Jesus I pray. (Reference Scriptures: Romans 12:15, Romans 15:1-2, 1 Corinthians 14:3, 2 Corinthians 1:3-4, Colossians 3:16)

I decree, declare, and pray that my speech and conversations are full of grace in the name of Jesus I pray. (Reference Scripture: Colossians 4:6)

I decree, declare, and pray that I intentionally excel in gifts that build up others especially those in the church in the name of Jesus I pray. (Reference Scriptures: Romans 14:19, Romans 15:2, Ephesians 4:29)

I decree, declare, and pray that my mind is blessed and fruitful with the things of God in the name of Jesus I pray. (Reference Scriptures: Romans 12:2, Colossians 3:1-17)

I decree, declare, and pray that I weigh carefully what others say and I listen thoroughly before answering in the name of Jesus I pray. (Reference Scripture: Proverbs 18:13)

I decree, declare, and pray that I do everything in a fitting and orderly way. I love God's order in the name of Jesus I pray. (Reference Scriptures: 1 Corinthians 14:40, 1 Corinthians 14:33)

I decree, declare, and pray that I consistently develop the fruit of joy. The joy of the Lord is my strength. I confess joy, I live by joy, and I enjoy joy's power in the name of Jesus I pray. (Reference Scriptures: Nehemiah 8:10, Psalms 5:11, Psalms 27:1, Proverbs 17:22, Isaiah 41:13, Romans 15:13, Galatians 5:22, Philippians 4:4)

I decree, declare, and pray that I have Divine victory in all areas of my life in the name of Jesus I pray. (Reference Scripture: 1 Corinthians 15:57)

I decree, declare, and pray that I draw on the supply of the Holy Spirit that's within me and I come out on top in the name of Jesus I pray. (Reference Scriptures: Isaiah 26:3, Matthew 10:19-20, Luke 12:12, John 1:1-4, John 14:15-17, John 14:26, John 3:34, Acts 1:8, 1 Corinthians 10:13, Galatians 3:5, Galatians 4:6, Ephesians 4:30, Ephesians 5:18, 1 John 3:22-23, Jude 1:20-21)

I decree, declare, and pray that God arms me with strength and makes my way perfect in the name of Jesus I pray. (Reference Scripture: Psalms 18:32)

I decree, declare, and pray that I receive and I achieve favorable results in every area of my life because greater is my God in me than anything else in the world in the name of Jesus I pray. (Reference Scriptures: Psalms 5:12, Psalms 23:5-6, Psalms 30:5, Proverbs 3:3-4, Mark 11:24, 2 Corinthians 9:8, Ephesians 1:17-18, Philippians 4:19, Hebrews 4:16, 1 John 4:4)

I decree, declare, and pray that my Lord Jesus Christ Himself, and my God and Father has loved me and given me everlasting consolation and good hope by grace, He comforts my heart and establishes me in every good word and work in the name of Jesus I pray. (Reference Scriptures: 2 Thessalonians 2:16-17)

I decree, declare, and pray that God makes all grace abound toward me and I always have all sufficiency in all things having an abundance for every good work in the name of Jesus I pray. (Reference Scripture: 2 Corinthians 9:8)

I decree, declare, and pray that God has redeemed my life from destruction, crowned me with loving kindness and tender mercies. God satisfies my mouth with good things and my youth is renewed like the eagles in the name of Jesus I pray. (Reference Scriptures: Psalms 103:4-5)

I decree, declare, and pray that God has crowned me with glory and honor. God has made me to have dominion over the works of His hands and has put all things under my feet in the name of Jesus I pray. (Reference Scriptures: Psalms 8:4-6)

I decree, declare, and pray that I receive divine interception in all things because God orders His angels to protect me in all my ways in the name of Jesus I pray. (Reference Scriptures: Job 36:11, Psalms 75:6-7, Psalms 91:9-12, Proverbs 3:5-6, Proverbs 8:35, Proverbs 16:7, Isaiah 1:19, Daniel 10:10-14, John 14:21, Romans 8:28, Hebrews 5:9, Jude 1:20, Jude 1:24-25)

I decree, declare, and pray that I am happy, joyful, and glad. I stay in a state of rejoicing with God because I keep my mind on Him and no weapon formed against me shall prosper in the name of Jesus I pray. (Reference Scriptures: Psalms 35:27, Psalms 146:5, Isaiah 23:3, Isaiah 54:17, Romans 8:32, Philippians 4:4, 3 John 1:2)

I decree, declare, and pray that I practice obedience to God's principles, which makes me successful in my ways in the name of Jesus I pray. (Reference Scriptures: Joshua 1:8, Nehemiah 1:11, Psalms 1:1-3, Psalms 35:27, Psalms 37:4, Psalms 37:34, Proverbs 2:7, Proverbs 3:1-6, Proverbs 10:22, Proverbs 13:22, Proverbs 16:3, Ecclesiastes 5:19, Jeremiah 17:7, Jeremiah 29:11, Luke 16:10, Romans 8:32, 3 John 1:2)

I decree, declare, and pray that I am anointed from the Holy One to perceive and to know all things, knowing the truth in the name of Jesus I pray. (Reference Scripture: 1 John 2:20)

I decree, declare, and pray that I am blessed in the name of Jesus I pray. (Reference Scriptures: Deuteronomy 28:1-14, Job 5:17, Psalms 118:26, Psalms 146:5, Jeremiah 17:7, Matthew 5:1-16, Luke 11:28, John 1:16, 2 Corinthians 9:8, Ephesians 1:3-7, James 1:25, Revelation 1:3)

I decree, declare, and pray that I desire to have fresh encounters with God and a renewed call on my life. Thank You Lord God for stretching forth Your arm and hand in my favor in the name of Jesus I pray. (Reference Scriptures: Numbers 6:24-26, Deuteronomy 5:15, 1 Kings 8:41-43, Psalms 23:3, Psalms 34:18, Psalms 51:10, Psalms 51:12, Psalms 145:18, Proverbs 8:17, Isaiah 58:11, John 4:14, John 7:37-38, John 10:10, 2 Corinthians 13:9)

I decree, declare, and pray that the entire body of Christ have a fresh encounter with God and a renewed call. Thank You Lord God for stretching forth Your arm and hand in favor of Christians, Believers, and the Beloved Saints all over the world in the name of Jesus I pray. (Reference Scriptures: Numbers 6:24-26, Deuteronomy 5:15, 1 Kings 8:41-43, Psalms 23:3, Psalms 34:18, Psalms 51:10, Psalms 51:12, Psalms 145:18, Proverbs 8:17, Isaiah 58:11, John 4:14, John 7:37-38, John 10:10, 2 Corinthians 13:9, Ephesians 6:18, 1 Timothy 2:1, James 5:16)

CHAPTER TWO

FINANCIAL
DECREES, DECLARES & PRAYERS

**The tongue has the power
of life and death.**

Proverbs 18:21

**Thou shalt also decree a thing, and it
shall be established unto thee: and
the light shall shine upon thy ways.**

Job 22:28

**I decree, declare, and pray that every
good and perfect gift comes down from
the Father of light; therefore, today shall
end good and it shall end perfect
in Jesus' name I pray!**

James 1:17

I decree, declare, and pray that the wealth of the sinner is laid up for me because I am the righteousness of God in Jesus name I pray. (Reference Scriptures: Proverbs 13:22, 2 Corinthians 5:21)

I decree, declare, and pray that my hands are diligent in all my affairs and I bear rule as a child of God in the name of Jesus I pray. (Reference Scripture: Proverbs 12:24)

I decree, declare, and pray that God has given me the power to get wealth. I apply His ways to my life and live a life of gratitude towards Him in the name of Jesus I pray. (Reference Scripture: Deuteronomy 8:18)

I decree, declare, and pray that wealth and riches are in my house in the name of Jesus I pray. (Reference Scriptures: Psalms 112:1-3)

I decree, declare, and pray that I am a faithful steward over everything God has given me in the name of Jesus I pray. (Reference Scriptures: Matthew 25:14-30)

I decree, declare, and pray that when I am given opportunities to help others in their distress I respond promptly in my giving in the name of Jesus I pray. (Reference Scriptures: Philippians 4:10-20)

I decree, declare, and pray that I wisely navigate my streams of income with an anointing for business savvy in the name of Jesus I pray. (Reference Scripture: Proverbs 22:29)

I decree, declare, and pray that I am a lender and a generous giver in the name of Jesus I pray. (Reference Scriptures: Deuteronomy 15:6, Deuteronomy 28:12, Proverbs 22:7, Luke 6:38)

I decree, declare, and pray that I trust God and I lean not on my own understanding, in all my ways I acknowledge the Lord and He directs my paths in the name of Jesus I pray. (Reference Scriptures: Psalms 3:5-6, Proverbs 3:5-6)

I decree, declare, and pray that I consistently honor the Lord with my finances and all that I do and say in the name of Jesus I pray. (Reference Scriptures: 1 Samuel 2:30, Proverbs 3:9-11, Proverbs 4:7, Proverbs 10:11-14)

I decree, declare, and pray that I live within and below my means managing my finances efficiently in the name of Jesus I pray. (Reference Scriptures: Proverbs 13:22, Proverbs 21:20, Proverbs 22:7, Proverbs 27:23, Luke 12:15, Luke 14:28, Luke 16:11, Romans 13:8, James 1:5)

I decree, declare, and pray that I am a cheerful giver always listening for the guidance of the Holy Spirit's promptings to give and for what amount I give in the name of Jesus I pray. (Reference Scriptures: Matthews 6:2-4, 2 Corinthians 9:7)

I decree, declare, and pray that I am a discerning giver, never compulsive or reluctant in the name of Jesus I pray. (Reference Scripture: 2 Corinthians 9:7)

I decree, declare, and pray that God is able to make all grace abound toward me and I always have all sufficiency in all things having an abundance for every good work in Jesus name I pray. (Reference Scripture: 2 Corinthians 9:8)

I decree, declare, and pray that I put up a resistance towards procrastination in managing my financial affairs in the name of Jesus I pray. (Reference Scriptures: Proverbs 18:9, Ecclesiastes 11:4-6)

I decree, declare, and pray that I am debt free, I have excellent credit, and all my bills are paid on time in the name of Jesus I pray. (Reference Scriptures: Proverbs 22:7, Romans 13:8)

I decree, declare, and pray that I resist laziness. I work with prudence. I am far from poverty and lack because all my needs are met in the name of Jesus I pray. (Reference Scriptures: Proverbs 6:6-8, Proverbs 20:4, Proverbs 22:7, Proverbs 24:33-34, Proverbs 8:12, Matthew 6:33, Philippians 4:19)

I decree, declare, and pray that I am creative with my budget, wasting nothing in the name of Jesus I pray. (Reference Scriptures: Proverbs 27:23, John 6:12, 1 Timothy 6:17-19)

I decree, declare, and pray that I am diligent in all my financial dealings, money management skills, and I practice wise stewardship over all my possessions in the name of Jesus I pray. (Reference Scriptures: Proverbs 13:22, Matthew 25:1-30)

I decree, declare, and pray that my will works in perfect harmony with God's will as I am transformed into His dear son Jesus Christ in the name of Jesus I pray. (Reference Scriptures: Romans 12:2, Ephesians 5:1-21)

I decree, declare, and pray that I understand my times and seasons spending accordingly in the name of Jesus I pray. (Reference Scriptures: Psalms 39:4, Ecclesiastes 3:1-14)

I decree, declare, and pray that I recognize the transitory times in my life in the name of Jesus I pray. (Reference Scripture: Psalms 39:4)

I decree, declare, and pray that I manage the talents that God has given me according to His ways in the name of Jesus I pray. (Reference Scripture: Matthew 25:14)

I decree, declare, and pray that I am a faithful steward in both the small and large things in the name of Jesus I pray. (Reference Scriptures: Matthew 25:21, Luke 16:10)

I decree, declare, and pray that the favor of the Lord surrounds me in all things. I am blessed beyond measure in the name of Jesus I pray. (Reference Scriptures: Psalms 5:12, Colossians 1:21-22)

I decree, declare, and pray that I exercise my gifts, talents, and resources in the time God has allotted to me. (Reference Scriptures: Luke 19:12-27)

I decree, declare, and pray that the Lord is my Sheppard I shall not be in want in the name of Jesus I pray. (Reference Scripture: Psalms 23:1)

I decree, declare, and pray that I deal generously with others, lending, and conducting my affairs with justice in the name of Jesus I pray. (Reference Scripture: Psalms 112:5)

I decree, declare, and pray that I am diligent with managing money in the name of Jesus I pray. (Reference Scripture: Proverbs 10:4)

I decree, declare, and pray that I practice fairness and honesty towards others in the name of Jesus I pray. (Reference Scripture: Proverbs 11:1)

I decree, declare, and pray that I have drive, initiative, take action now approach, and work smart habits which creates daily increases in my life in the name of Jesus I pray. (Reference Scripture: Proverbs 13:11)

I decree, declare, and pray that I am wise, watchful and prepared. I count the cost of my choices before making them in the name of Jesus I pray. (Reference Scriptures: Luke 14:28-30)

I decree, declare, and pray that I save wisely for my future in the name of Jesus I pray. (Reference Scriptures: Proverbs 6:6-8, Proverbs 21:20)

I decree, declare, and pray that I practice godliness with contentment concerning money and possessions in the name of Jesus I pray. (Reference Scripture: 1 Timothy 6:6)

I decree, declare, and pray that through Christ strength I can do all things in the name of Jesus I pray. (Reference Scripture: Philippians 4:13)

I decree, declare, and pray that I practice being disciplined in my finances and I increase in my financial management knowledge seeing what pleases the Lord in the name of Jesus I pray. (Reference Scriptures: Proverbs 12:1, Ephesians 5:10-11)

I decree, declare, and pray that I have mastery over my fleshly desires, thoughts, words, and actions. I cast down every imagination and thought that exalts itself against the knowledge of God bringing every thought into the captivity to the obedience of Christ. I wear the helmet of salvation in the name of Jesus I pray. (Reference Scriptures: 2 Corinthians 10:2-6, Ephesians 6:17)

I decree, declare, and pray that I have all of heavens resources made available to me when I need them in the name of Jesus I pray. (Reference Scriptures: Psalms 37:25-26, Matthew 6:33, 2 Timothy 1:7)

I decree, declare, and pray that I do everything in a fitting and orderly way in the name of Jesus I pray. (Reference Scriptures: 1 Corinthians 14:40, 1 Corinthians 14:33)

I decree, declare and pray that God supplies all my needs according to His riches and glory which have been given to me in Christ Jesus in the name of Jesus I pray. (Reference Scripture: Philippians 4:19)

I decree, declare, and pray that I am very successful in the name of Jesus I pray. (Reference Scriptures: Joshua 1:8, Jeremiah 17:7, Jeremiah 29:11, Psalms 35:27, Proverbs 10:22, Proverbs 13:22, Ecclesiastes 5:19, Romans 8:32, Ephesians 6:17, 3 John 1:2)

I decree, declare and pray that God is able to keep me from falling and present me blameless in the presence of His glory with exceeding joy in all that I face throughout my day in the name of Jesus I pray. (Reference Scripture: Jude 1:24)

I decree, declare, and pray that I am blessed in the name of Jesus I pray. (Reference Scriptures: Jeremiah 17:7, Psalms 107:2, Psalms 118:26, Proverbs 10:22, Matthew 23:39, Matthew 5:1-12, Ephesians 2:8)

I decree, declare and pray that all of my help comes from the Lord in the name of Jesus I pray. (Reference Scriptures: Psalms 121:1-8)

I decree, declare, and pray that I put up resistance against a poverty mindset. I focus on possibilities because God supplies all my needs in the name of Jesus I pray. (Reference Scripture: Philippians 4:19)

I decree, declare, and pray that I receive a good harvest from the good seeds I have sown. I sow finances into the kingdom of God consistently helping others in the body of Christ do the work of the Lord. Therefore, I am daily loaded down with benefits and blessings in the name of Jesus I pray. (Reference Scriptures: Psalms 68:19, 2 Corinthians 9:6-7, Galatians 6:7)

CHAPTER THREE

HEALTH RELATED
DECREES, DECLARES & PRAYERS

**The tongue has the power
of life and death.**

Proverbs 18:21

**Thou shalt also decree a thing, and it
shall be established unto thee: and
the light shall shine upon thy ways.**

Job 22:28

**I decree, declare, and pray that every
good and perfect gift comes down from
the Father of light; therefore, today shall
end good and it shall end perfect
in Jesus' name I pray!**

James 1:17

A sound heart is the life of the flesh, but envy the rottenness of the bones. (Reference Scripture: Proverbs 14:30)

I decree, declare, and pray that my mind is in perfect peace because I trust in the Lord in the name of Jesus I pray. (Reference Scripture: Isaiah 26:3)

I decree, declare, and pray that whatever comes my way will be alright because I am saved. I know my future is secure because I am in the safety of God's hands and when I die I'll be standing before Him receiving the crown of life because I love God and believe in His Son Jesus Christ in the name of Jesus I pray. (Reference Scriptures: Psalms 4:8, Proverbs 19:23, Proverbs 21:31, Joshua 1:9, Jeremiah 29:11, Romans 8:18, Philippians 1:6, James 1:12)

I decree, declare, and pray that I am quick to hear, slow to speak and slow to anger. I choose to forgive others of their wrongdoings against me and walk in love towards all in the name of Jesus I pray. (Reference Scriptures: Matthew 6:14-15, 1 Corinthians 13:1-7, Ephesians 4:32, Colossians 3:13, James 1:19-20)

I decree, declare, and pray that God restores my health as I choose to forgive others of their debts towards me in the name of Jesus I pray. (Reference Scriptures: Psalms 38, Jeremiah 30:17, 3 John 1:2)

I decree, declare, and pray that I discipline my body and bring it into subjection of the Holy Spirit in the name of Jesus I pray. (Reference Scriptures: 1 Corinthians 9:24-27, James 3:1-2)

I decree, declare, and pray that when I go to bed my sleep is sound, restful, restoring, sweet, and healing because I forgive others of their wrongs and I walk in wisdom in the name of Jesus I pray. (Reference Scriptures: Proverbs 3:24, Matthew 6:14)

I decree, declare, and pray that my physical body is strong, resilient, healthy and well in the name of Jesus I pray. (Reference Scriptures: Psalms 119:28, Isaiah 40:29-31, 1 Corinthians 6:19-20, 1 Timothy 4:8)

I decree, declare, and pray that I am healthy and strong, sickness and diseases are far from me in the name of Jesus I pray. (Reference Scriptures: Exodus 15:26, Exodus 23:25, Deuteronomy 7:15, Psalms 103:1-5)

I decree, declare, and pray that God is my Great Physician; I walk in wellness, strength, energy, and vitality in the name of Jesus I pray. (Reference Scriptures: Psalms 54:4, Matthew 9:12-13)

I decree, declare, and pray that I am happy and energetic in the name of Jesus I pray. (Reference Scriptures: Psalms 103:1-2)

I decree, declare, and pray that I am quick to repent, God restores my health, I utter only worthy words over my life in the name of Jesus I pray. (Reference Scripture: Jeremiah 15:19)

I decree, declare, and pray I take daily actions to improve the quality of my physical and mental health in the name of Jesus I pray. (Reference Scriptures: Proverbs 18:9, 1 Corinthians 2:16, Ephesians 5:16- 17)

I decree, declare, and pray that I am strong and powerful in the name of Jesus I pray. (Reference Scriptures: Psalms 23:4, Isaiah 41:10, Philippians 4:11, James 4:7, 1 Peter 5:7)

I decree, declare, and pray that I put up resistance against depression and hopelessness because my hope is in the Lord. Greater is He that is in me. The joy of the Lord is my strength in the name of Jesus I pray. (Reference Scriptures: Nehemiah 8:10, Psalms 5:11, Psalms 28:7, Psalms 39:7, Isaiah 41:10, 1 John 4:4)

I decree, declare, and pray that the duration of my faith is strong, steadfast, and fights until the end. I am more than a conqueror through Christ Jesus who loves me unconditionally in the name of Jesus I pray. (Reference Scripture: Romans 8:37)

I decree, declare, and pray that every part of my body operates the way God designed it to function because I am wonderfully made in the name of Jesus I pray. (Reference Scripture: Psalms 139:14)

I decree, declare, and pray that I have a healthy body; I intentionally choose to eat more nutritious foods in the name of Jesus I pray. (Reference Scriptures: Job 22:28, Psalms 103:5, Proverbs 4:7)

I decree, declare, and pray that I have a cheerful heart in the name of Jesus I pray. (Reference Scripture: Proverbs 17:22)

I decree, declare, and pray that I reposition myself for all God has for me to do concerning my physical health. I purposely and intentionally improve the quality of my health in the name of Jesus I pray. (Reference Scriptures: Psalms 139:1-24, Matthew 19:26, Mark 10:27)

I decree, declare, and pray that I am very creative in managing my time and health needs in the name of Jesus I pray. (Reference Scriptures: Ecclesiastes 3:1-8)

I decree, declare, and pray that I think things through concerning eating and living a healthier lifestyle in the name of Jesus I pray. (Reference Scriptures: Proverbs 21:5, Philippians 4:8, 1 Corinthians 14:40)

I decree, declare, and pray that I find pleasure in understanding the truth about my health in the name of Jesus I pray. (Reference Scripture: Proverbs 17:28)

I decree, declare, and pray that I honor God with my body in the name of Jesus I pray. (Reference Scriptures: 1 Corinthians 6:19-20, 2 Timothy 1:12)

I decree, declare, and pray that I have the funds to take care of my mental and physical health at all times in the name of Jesus I pray. (Reference Scriptures: Matthew 7:7-8, Philippians 4:19, Jude 1:24)

I decree, declare, and pray that my hope is in the Lord. I will fear no one and no thing in the name of Jesus I pray. (Reference Scriptures: Psalms 118:6, Psalms 131:3, Hebrews 13:6)

I decree, declare, and pray that I love discipline and knowledge in the name of Jesus I pray. (Reference Scripture: Proverbs 12:1)

I decree, declare, and pray that I know how to see, I have self awareness. I am fully aware of my potential and what is possible in the world around me in the name of Jesus I pray. (Reference Scriptures: Proverbs 14:8, Matthew 19:26, Romans 12:3, Galatians 6:3, 2 Peter 1:1-15)

I decree, declare, and pray that I know how to align my actions to my desired outcomes. I meet my objectives and I follow through consistently in the name of Jesus I pray. (Reference Scriptures: Proverbs 14:8, Matthew 16:24-25, 2 Peter 1:1-15)

I decree, declare, and pray that I am able to stand against the wiles, tricks, and schemes of the devil in the name of Jesus I pray. (Reference Scriptures: Matthew 16:23, 2 Corinthians 2:10-11, Jude 1:9, Ephesians 6:10-18, James 4:7, 1 John 2:16, 1 John 4:1)

I decree, declare, and pray that I am self-controlled in the name of Jesus I pray. (Reference Scriptures: Galatians 5:22-23)

I decree, declare, and pray that I am joyful. (Reference Scriptures: Galatians 5:22-23)

I decree, declare, and pray that I am kind in the name of Jesus I pray. (Reference Scriptures: Galatians 5:22-23)

I decree, declare, and pray that I am patient in the name of Jesus I pray. (Reference Scriptures: Galatians 5:22-23)

I decree, declare, and pray that I am compassionate in the name of Jesus I pray. (Reference Scriptures: Galatians 5:22-23)

I decree, declare, and pray that I am a loving person in the name of Jesus I pray. (Reference Scriptures: Galatians 5:22-23)

I decree, declare, and pray that I am a forgiving person in the name of Jesus I pray. (Reference Scriptures: Galatians 5:22-23)

I decree, declare, and pray that I am a peaceful person in the name of Jesus I pray. (Reference Scriptures: Galatians 5:22-23)

I decree, declare, and pray that I am more than a conqueror, having victory in all things in the name of Jesus I pray. (Reference Scripture: Romans 8:37)

I decree, declare, and pray that I think on things that are true, possible, honorable, just, lovely, praise worthy, of a good report, and virtuous in the name of Jesus I pray. (Reference Scripture: Philippians 4:8)

I decree, declare, and pray that I serve the Lord wholeheartedly. He blesses my food and water, taking away all my sicknesses in the name of Jesus I pray. (Reference Scripture: Exodus 23:25)

I decree, declare, and pray that God delivers me out of all my afflictions and destructions in the name of Jesus I pray. (Reference Scriptures: Psalms 34:19, Psalms 107:20)

I decree, declare, and pray that I am spiritually and physically healthy. No weapon formed against me shall prosper in the name of Jesus I pray. (Reference Scriptures: I Chronicles 29:11-13, Joshua 1:8, Jeremiah 17:7, Jeremiah 29:11, Psalms 107:20, Isaiah 54:17, Matthew 14:14, Acts 10:38, Romans 8:32, Ephesians 6:17, 1 Peter 2:24, 3 John 1:2)

I decree, declare, and pray that I am happy and excited. My spirit is ignited with wonderful anticipations in the name of Jesus I pray. (Reference Scriptures: Joshua 1:8, Jeremiah 17:7, Jeremiah 29:11, Psalms 16:20, Psalms 35:27, Romans 8:32, Ephesians 6:17, 3 John 1:2)

I decree, declare, and pray that I am healed in the name of Jesus I pray. (Reference Scripture: Isaiah 53:5)

I decree, declare, and pray that I victoriously fight and overcome spirits of heaviness, depression, oppression, and despair by putting on the garment of praise. Speaking words of praise and thankfulness, singing to God, thanking Jesus for His shed blood for me in the name of Jesus I pray. (Reference: Psalms 19:7-11, Psalms 149:4-6, Isaiah 61:3)

I decree, declare, and pray that I call on the name of the Lord and He restores my health and heals all my wounds in the name of Jesus I pray. (Reference Scripture: Jeremiah 30:17)

CHAPTER FOUR

THE MIND
DECREES, DECLARES & PRAYERS

**The tongue has the power
of life and death.**

Proverbs 18:21

**Thou shalt also decree a thing, and it
shall be established unto thee: and
the light shall shine upon thy ways.**

Job 22:28

**I decree, declare, and pray that every
good and perfect gift comes down from
the Father of light; therefore, today shall
end good and it shall end perfect
in Jesus' name I pray!**

James 1:17

I decree, declare, and pray that I am being conformed and patterned after the Kingdom of God and my mind is renewed today in the name of Jesus I pray. (Reference Scripture: Romans 12:2)

I decree, declare, and pray that I reposition myself for all God has for me to do in the name of Jesus I pray. (Reference Scriptures: Jeremiah 1:5, Philippians 3:13-15)

I decree, declare, and pray that my mind is strong and resolute. I keep a positive mindset through the challenges I encounter because no weapon formed against me shall prosper in the name of Jesus I pray. (Reference Scriptures: Isaiah 54:17, Jeremiah 29:11, Matthew 15:11, 1 Corinthians 2:16, Philippians 4:6, Philippians 4:8)

I decree, declare, and pray that I overcome depression, oppression and despair by putting on the garment of praise. Singing praises to God for everything He has done for me in the name of Jesus I pray. (Reference Scriptures: Psalms 19:7-11, Psalms 149:4-6, Isaiah 61:3)

I decree, declare, and pray that I carefully consider and monitor my behavior before the Lord in the name of Jesus I pray. (Reference Scriptures: Leviticus 20:26, Proverbs 5:21, Haggai 1:7, Ephesians 5:1-2, Ephesians 5:8-10, 1 Peter 1:13-16)

I decree, declare, and pray that I am mindful of how I am perceived by others. I consistently practice discipline and diligence in all my dealings, management, and stewardships in the name of Jesus I pray. (Reference Scriptures: Proverbs 22:29, Matthew 16:26, 1 Corinthians 16:13, Ephesians 5:1-2, Ephesians 5:8-10, 1 Thessalonians 4:9-12)

I decree, declare, and pray that my will works in perfect harmony with God's will in the name of Jesus I pray. (Reference Scriptures: James 4:7, 1 Peter 5:6, Ephesians 5:1-21, Ephesians 6:1-24)

I decree, declare, and pray that I recognize the transitory seasons in my life. I understand what to do during my time and seasons because God's mighty power is at work in me in the name of Jesus I pray. (Reference Scriptures: Psalms 31:15, Ecclesiastes 3:1-8, Ephesians 1:17-19, Ephesians 5:1-21)

I decree, declare, and pray that I am mindful and have a passion for the things God calls important in the name of Jesus I pray. (Reference Scriptures: Matthew 5:6, Matthew 22:37-39, Luke 2:49, John 5:19, John 6:38, Ephesians 5:1-21, Hebrews 11:24-26)

I decree, declare, and pray that the Holy Spirit renews my thoughts and attitudes. My mind is renewed and empowered in the name of Jesus I pray. (Reference Scriptures: Ephesians 4:23-24)

I decree, declare, and pray that I am the light of the world and the salt of the earth. I live as a child of God consisting of all goodness, righteousness, and truth. I find out and do what pleases the Lord in the name of Jesus I pray. (Reference Scriptures: Matthew 5:13-16, Ephesians 5:8-10)

I decree, declare, and pray that I am diligent to the very end making my hope sure in the name of Jesus I pray. (Reference Scriptures: 1 Corinthians 9:24-27, 1 Timothy 6:12, Hebrews 12:1, Hebrews 6:11)

I decree, declare, and pray that I am mindful that I am a child of God. I love who I am, who God has created me to be, and I live authentically every day in the name of Jesus I pray. (Reference Scriptures: Jeremiah 29:11, Psalms 139:14, James 1:22-25, James 2:26)

I decree, declare, and pray that I am fully aware and fully integrated to what God has called me to do. I am mentally prepared because I have the mind of Christ in the name of Jesus I pray. (Reference Scriptures: Psalms 119:1-12, Luke 21:27-28, 1 Corinthians 2:16, Colossians 2:6, 10, 1 Peter 1:13, Revelation 16:15)

I decree, declare, and pray that I always see the possibilities in myself and my God given potential in the name of Jesus I pray. (Reference Scriptures: Jeremiah 29:11, Psalms 139:14, Romans 8:28, Romans 8:37, Philippians 4:13, 1 Peter 3:12)

I decree, declare, and pray that I am very successful in the name of Jesus I pray. (Reference Scriptures: Joshua 1:8, Jeremiah 17:7, Jeremiah 29:11, Psalms 35:27, Proverbs 10:22, Proverbs 13:22, Ecclesiastes 5:19, Romans 8:32, Ephesians 6:17, 3 John 1:2)

I decree, declare, and pray that I can truly see the best in myself and others in the name of Jesus I pray. (Reference Scriptures: Matthew 7:1-5, John 13:34-35, Romans 8:28, Philippians 4:13, 1 John 4:7-8)

I decree, declare, and pray that I align my actions to my desired outcomes and objectives consistently following through. I am tough-minded in the name of Jesus I pray. (Reference Scriptures: Numbers 30:2, Joshua 1:9, Psalms 37:4, Ecclesiastes 5:4-5, Ecclesiastes 7:8, Luke 14:28-33, 1 Corinthians 16:13, Philippians 1:6)

I decree, declare, and pray that I stand against the wiles, tricks, and schemes of the devil in the name of Jesus I pray. (Reference Scriptures: Matthew 16:23, 2 Corinthians 2:10-11, Jude 1:9, Ephesians 6:10-18, James 4:7, 1 John 2:16, 1 John 4:1)

I decree, declare, and pray that I operate accurately in the power of God with a sound mind, mental clarity, and love in the name of Jesus I pray. (Reference Scripture: 2 Timothy 1:7)

I decree, declare, and pray that I consistently practice mastery over my fleshly desires, thoughts, words, and deeds. I speak and agree with the Word of God, casting down every imagination and thought that exalts itself against the knowledge of God bringing every thought into the captivity to the obedience of Christ Jesus in the name of Jesus I pray. (Reference Scriptures: Romans 6:6-14, 2 Corinthians 10:2-6, Galatians 5:16-18)

I decree, declare, and pray that I am worthy of all that God has for me because of what Jesus did for me in the name of Jesus I pray. (Reference Scriptures: Matthew 10:31, John 3:16, Romans 8:1-4, Romans 8:28, 2 Corinthians 12:9, Ephesians 2:4-10, Ephesians 3:14-21, Titus 3:4-7, Hebrews 4:16, Revelation 3:4-6)

I decree, declare, and pray that I walk in wisdom in the name of Jesus I pray. (Reference Scriptures: Job 12:12-13, Proverbs 3:13-18, Proverbs 4:7, Proverbs 19:20, Ecclesiastes 10:10, James 1:5, James 3:17)

I decree, declare, and pray that I get understanding of the ways of God in the name of Jesus I pray. (Reference Scriptures: Psalms 119:130, Proverbs 2:2-5, Proverbs 14:29)

I decree, declare, and pray that I am mentally competent in the name of Jesus I pray. (Reference: Proverbs 3:21-26, 2 Corinthians 3:5, Hebrews 13:20-21)

I decree, declare, and pray that I have a strong mind. I have the mind of Christ working through me in the name of Jesus I pray. (Reference Scriptures: Matthew 22:37, Romans 12:22, 1 Corinthians 2:16, James 1:2-4, 2 Timothy 1:7, 1 Peter 1:13, 1 John 4:18)

I decree, declare, and pray that I am intellectual operating in the knowledge of God in the name of Jesus I pray. (Reference Scriptures: John 14:26, John 15:26, John 17:17, 1 Corinthians 14:22, 1 Thessalonians 5:21, 2 Timothy 1:6-7)

I decree, declare, and pray that my brain works and functions according to God's design in the name of Jesus I pray. (Reference Scriptures: 2 Corinthians 5:17, Philippians 2:13, Ephesians 2:10)

I decree, declare, and pray that I guard my mind and heart in the name of Jesus I pray. (Reference Scriptures: Proverbs 4:23, Proverbs 4:20-27)

I decree, declare, and pray that my mind mediates and thinks on things that are true, possible, honorable, just, lovely, praise worthy, of a good report, and virtuous in the name of Jesus I pray. (Reference Scriptures: Philippians 4:8-9)

CHAPTER FIVE

CAREER, WORK RELATED
DECREES, DECLARES & PRAYERS

**The tongue has the power
of life and death.**

Proverbs 18:21

**Thou shalt also decree a thing, and it
shall be established unto thee: and
the light shall shine upon thy ways.**

Job 22:28

**I decree, declare, and pray that every
good and perfect gift comes down from
the Father of light; therefore, today shall
end good and it shall end perfect
in Jesus' name I pray!**

James 1:17

Iron sharpens iron, and one man sharpens another. (Reference Scripture: Proverbs 27:17)

I decree, declare, and pray that God blesses the works of my hands in Jesus name I pray. (Reference Scriptures: Deuteronomy 15:10, Psalms 90:17)

I decree, declare, and pray that whatever circumstances I am facing today, I am full of joy and I am strong in the Lord and in the power of His might in the name of Jesus I pray. (Reference Scriptures: Nehemiah 8:10, Psalms 5:11, John 16:24, Romans 15:13, Ephesians 6:10, James 1:2-5)

I decree, declare, and pray that I practice honesty, integrity, truthfulness, and I get along peacefully with others in the name of Jesus I pray. (Reference Scriptures: Exodus 20:16, Proverbs 11:27, Proverbs 12:22, Matthew 5:16, Matthew 6:12-15, John 13:34, Romans 12:18, 1 Thessalonians 4:9-12, 1 Peter 3:10-12, 1 Peter 5:2-7, Hebrews 12:14-15, Hebrews 13:18)

I decree, declare, and pray that I have impeccable work ethics in the name of Jesus I pray. (Reference Scriptures: Proverbs 10:4, Proverbs 12:11, Proverbs 12:24, Proverbs 14:23, Proverbs 16:3, Ecclesiastes 9:10, Colossians 3:23, 1 Thessalonians 4:11-12, 1 Timothy 5:8, 2 Timothy 2:15)

I decree, declare, and pray that I have discernment and walk in wisdom in all my dealings, management, and stewardships in the name of Jesus I pray. (Reference Scriptures: Proverbs 10:4, Proverbs 11:3, Proverbs 16:3, Proverbs 22:29, 2 Corinthians 8:21, 1 Thessalonians 4:9-12, 1 Timothy 5:8, 1 Peter 5:3-5)

I decree, declare, and pray that I have a thirst for doing things God's way in the name of Jesus I pray. (Reference Scriptures: Proverbs 10:22, Romans 12:1-21, 1 Corinthians 10:31, Colossians 3:23, 1 Thessalonians 4:9-12, 1 Timothy 5:8)

I decree, declare, and pray that I reposition myself for all God has for me to do in the name of Jesus I pray. (Reference Scriptures: Psalms 1:1-6, Proverbs 22:29)

I decree, declare, and pray that I follow orders and do my best work as unto the Lord in the name of Jesus I pray. (Reference Scriptures: Proverbs 10:22, Proverbs 13:4, Ecclesiastes 9:10, 1 Corinthians 10:31, 1 Corinthians 15:58, Colossians 3:17, 1 Thessalonians 4:9-12, 2 Timothy 2:1-7 The Message Bible Version, 1 Peter 5:3-5)

I decree, declare, and pray that I walk in wisdom understanding my times and seasons. I get my tasks done on time in the name of Jesus I pray. (Reference Scriptures: Psalms 31:15, Psalms 90:12, Proverbs 11:27, Proverbs 12:24, Ecclesiastes 3:1-8, Ecclesiastes 9:10, James 4:13-15, 2 Peter 3:8)

I decree, declare, and pray that I am a wise creative employee, worker, employer, business owner, and entrepreneur in the name of Jesus I pray. (Reference Scriptures: Deuteronomy 28:1-14, Joshua 1:8, Proverbs 4:7, Proverbs 10:4, Proverbs 10:22, Proverbs 12:24, Proverbs 13:4, Proverbs 22:29, Matthew 25:14-30, Galatians 6:9, 2 Timothy 2:15, 1 Peter 5:3-5)

I decree, declare, and pray that I am quick to hear, slow to speak, and slow to anger in the name of Jesus I pray. (Reference Scriptures: Proverbs 29:11, Proverbs 29:20, Ephesians 4:26, James 1:17-25)

I decree, declare, and pray that I am a great and loving communicator allowing others to finish speaking before answering them in the name of Jesus I pray. (Reference Scriptures: Proverbs 18:13, Proverbs 29:20, 1 Corinthians 13:4-5, 1 Corinthians 14:40, Philippians 2:3)

I decree, declare, and pray that I am fully aware of my potential and what is possible in the world around me in the name of Jesus I pray. (Reference Scriptures: Matthew 19:26, 2 Corinthians 5:17, 1 John 4:4, 1 Peter 2:9)

I decree, declare, and pray that I have the mind of Christ and I look out for the interests of others firsts then my own interests with pure motives and love in the name of Jesus I pray. (Reference Scriptures: 1 Corinthians 2:16, Philippians 2:1-5, 1 John 3:16)

I decree, declare, and pray that I am fully aware and awake to my potential, embracing each and every aspect of my identity, which is in Christ Jesus doing the job that is before me honorably in the name of Jesus I pray. (Reference Scriptures: Matthew 19:26, 2 Corinthians 5:17, Ephesians 2:10, 1 John 4:4, 1 Peter 2:9)

I decree, declare, and pray that I fully accept responsibility for my part of where I am now in my life. I can and I am changing for my own improvement in the name of Jesus I pray. (Reference Scriptures: Genesis 4:7, Numbers 32:23, Isaiah 3:10-11, Ezekiel 18:20, Romans 1:20, Romans 1:20-23 The Message Version, 1 Corinthians 13:11, Galatians 6:7-8, Philippians 4:13)

I decree, declare, and pray that I am able to break down the vision for my life into actionable steps reaching my full potential for the Lord in the name of Jesus I pray. (Reference Scriptures: Proverbs 29:18, Habakkuk 2:2-3, Ephesians 1:15-19 & Ephesians 1:15-19 The Message Bible Version, 2 Timothy 1:7, 2 Timothy 2:7, 1 John 4:4)

I decree, declare, and pray that I am energetic in my work in the name of Jesus I pray. (Reference Scriptures: Luke 15:7, John 21:25, Titus 3:2)

I decree, declare, and pray that I am always humble and appreciative in the name of Jesus I pray. (Reference Scripture: Proverbs 18:9)

I decree, declare, and pray that I am teachable in the name of Jesus I pray. (Reference Scriptures: Proverbs 12:1, Proverbs 18:13, 2 Timothy 3:16, 1 Peter 5:5)

I decree, declare, and pray that I manage my time well in the name of Jesus I pray. (Reference Scriptures: Psalms 39:4-5, Psalms 90:12, Proverbs 16:19, Ecclesiastes 3:1-14, Luke 14:28, Ephesians 5:15-17, Colossians 4:5, James 4:13-17)

I decree, declare, and pray that I am prosperous, living in the anointing that God has for me to increase my wisdom, understanding, productivity, diligence, discernment, knowledge and income in the name of Jesus I pray. (Reference Scriptures: Deuteronomy 28:8, Joshua 1:8, Psalms 1:1-3, Psalms 35:27, Psalms 45:7, Psalms 118:25, Proverbs 1:7, Proverbs 4:7, Proverbs 9:10, Proverbs 12:11, Proverbs 22:29, Proverbs 28:25, Nehemiah 1:11, John 10:10, John 16:13, 2 Corinthians 1:21-22, 1 John 2:27, 3 John 1:2)

I decree, declare, and pray that I am diligent in all my work assignments and job tasks in the name of Jesus I pray. (Reference Scriptures: Proverbs 10:4, Proverbs 13:4, Matthew 25:14-30, 2 Corinthians 8:21, 1 Thessalonians 4:10-12)

I decree, declare, and pray that I am gracious and diligent in my management skills with people and work assignments in the name of Jesus I pray.
(Reference Scriptures: Proverbs 10:4, Matthew 5:16, Matthew 25:14-30, Luke 19:12-27, Colossians 4:1-6, Ephesians 6:5-10)

I decree, declare, and pray that my will works in perfect harmony with God's will in the name of Jesus I pray. (Reference Scriptures: Deuteronomy 29:29, Romans 12:1-2, Ephesians 1:11, Ephesians 5:1-21, Ephesians 6:1-20, 1 Thessalonians 4:3-5 , 1 Thessalonians 5:18, 1 John 2:17 James 4:7, 1 Peter 5:6)

I decree, declare, and pray that I use my gifts, talents, and skills in the time available to me in the name of Jesus I pray. (Reference Scriptures: Psalms 90:12, Matthew 25:14-30 with emphasis on verses 14 -15, Luke 14:28, John 3:27, john 15:5, Romans 11:29, Romans 12:5-6, 1 Corinthians 12:4-7 and verse 11, James 1:17, 1 Peter 4:10)

I decree, declare, pray that I am fully aware as well as fully integrated to what God has called me to do in this season of my life in the name of Jesus I pray. (Reference Scriptures: Psalms 1:1-3, Psalms 139, Matthew 25:21, John 15:5, 1 Corinthians 9:24-25, Philippians 1:6, Colossians 3:1-4, Colossians 3:12-17, Colossians 3:23-24, Hebrews 12:1-3)

I decree, declare, and pray that I apply my God given potential. I see the possibilities in myself and I choose to move in that direction in the name of Jesus I pray. (Reference Scriptures: 1 Corinthians 9:24, 2 Corinthians 5:17, 1 John 4:4, 1 Peter 2:9)

I decree, declare, and pray that God has given me all things that pertain to life and godliness. I know how to align my actions to my desired outcomes, objectives, and I follow through consistently in the name of Jesus I pray. (Reference Scriptures: Proverbs 14:8, Matthew 16:24-25, 2 Peter 1:1-15)

I decree, declare, and pray that I am strong. I am powerful in the Lord's might. I clothe myself consistently in the whole armor of God able to stand against the wiles, tricks, and schemes of the devil. I am a blessing to my workplace in the name of Jesus I pray. (Reference Scriptures: Matthew 16:23, 2 Corinthians 2:10-11, Jude 1:9, Ephesians 6:10-18, James 4:7, 1 John 2:16, 1 John 4:1)

I decree, declare, and pray that I trust and take refuge in the Lord. **The Lord always helps, delivers, and saves me from the wicked in the name of Jesus I pray.** (Reference Scriptures: Psalms 37:39-40, Psalms 91:1-15)

I decree, declare, and pray that I do everything in a decent, fitting and orderly way in the name of Jesus I pray. (Reference Scriptures: 1 Corinthians 14:33, 1 Corinthians 14:40)

I decree, declare, and pray that I honor my boss, doing honest work with sincerity of heart in the name of Jesus I pray. (Reference Scriptures: Luke 16:10, Ephesians 6:5-8, Colossians 3:17, Colossians 3:22-24, 1 Peter 2:13-17, 1 Peter 2:18-23)

I decree, declare, and pray that I manage with integrity and I honor my employees with sincerity of heart in the name of Jesus I pray. (Reference Scriptures: Deuteronomy 16:19, Proverbs 11:1, Proverbs 28:18, Luke 6:31, Luke 16:10, Acts 24:16, Colossians 4:1, Colossians 3:17, Ephesians 6:8-9, 1 Peter 2:11-12)

I decree, declare, and pray that I treat my co-workers with honor, kindness, and sincerity of heart in the name of Jesus I pray. (Reference Scriptures: Matthew 7:12, Luke 6:31, John 15:12, Ephesians 4:29-32, Colossians 3:12-14, Colossians 3:22-24)

I decree, declare, and pray that I am full of good works, working very well with others bringing glory to God in the name of Jesus I pray. (Reference Scriptures: Matthew 5:16, Ephesians 4:28, 1 Thessalonians 4:9-12)

I decree, declare, and pray that I pursue honest work to earn my wages in the name of Jesus I pray.
(Reference Scriptures: Proverbs 12:11, Luke 10:7, Ephesians 2:8-10, Ephesians 4:28, 2 Thessalonians 3:6-12)

I decree, declare, and pray that God has established the works of my hands and His favor is resting on me in the name of Jesus I pray. (Reference Scriptures: Psalms 5:12, Psalms 30:5, Psalms 84:11, Psalms 90:17)

CHAPTER SIX

FAMILY RELATED
DECREES, DECLARES & PRAYERS

**The tongue has the power
of life and death.**

Proverbs 18:21

**Thou shalt also decree a thing, and it
shall be established unto thee: and
the light shall shine upon thy ways.**

Job 22:28

**I decree, declare, and pray that every
good and perfect gift comes down from
the Father of light; therefore, today shall
end good and it shall end perfect
in Jesus' name I pray!**

James 1:17

He who guards his mouth and his tongue keeps himself from troubles. (Reference Scripture: Proverbs 21:23)

I decree, declare, and pray that the favor of the Lord surrounds me and my family like a shield in the name of Jesus I pray. (Reference Scriptures: Psalms 5:12, Psalms 18:30)

I decree, declare, and pray that me and my family are safely protected by God in the name of Jesus I pray. (Reference Scriptures: Psalms 27:1, Psalms 91:1-2, Psalms 10:14-18, Proverbs 21:31 KJV ,2 Thessalonians 3:3)

I decree, declare, and pray that me and my family are respectful, compassionate, merciful, and forgiving of one another in the name of Jesus I pray. (Reference Scriptures: Matthew 5:7, John 13:34-35, Ephesians 4:32, Philippians 4:8, Colossians 3:13, Hebrews 4:16)

I decree, declare, and pray that I practice honor and unconditional love for my spouse in the name of Jesus I pray. (Reference Scriptures: John 13:34-35, 1 Corinthians 13:4 -7, Ephesians 5:1-2, Ephesians 5:21-33, Philippians 4:8, 1 Peter 4:8)

I decree, declare, and pray that I practice honoring and showing unconditional love towards my parents in the name of Jesus I pray. (Reference Scriptures: Exodus 20:12, Proverbs 20:20, Proverbs 23:22, John 13:34-35, Ephesians 6:1-3, Philippians 4:8)

I decree, declare, and pray that I practice discipline and unconditional love towards my children in the name of Jesus I pray. (Reference Scriptures: Proverbs 6:16-19, Proverbs 13:24, Proverbs 22:6, Proverbs 22:15, Proverbs 23:13, Proverbs 29:15, John 13:34-35, Ephesians 5:1, Ephesians 6:4, Philippians 4:8, 1 Peter 4:8)

I decree, declare, and pray that me and my family work together well, happily, and joyfully. The joy of the Lord is our strength in the name of Jesus I pray. (Reference Scriptures: Nehemiah 8:10, Psalms 16:11, Psalms 51:12, Proverbs 27:17, Ecclesiastes 4:9-12, John 15:4-5, Romans 15:5-6, 1 Corinthians 12:25-26, Philippians 4:8, 1, Colossians 3:24-24, Thessalonians 5:14-22)

I decree, declare, and pray that my family is blessed, wealth and riches are in my family's house in the name of Jesus I pray. (Reference Scriptures: Deuteronomy 8:18, Psalms 35:27, Psalms 36:7-8, Psalms 65:11, Psalms 68:19, Psalms 85:12, Psalms 112:1-3, Psalms 115:14, Proverbs 10:22, Proverbs 13:22, Jeremiah 17:7, 2 Corinthians 8:9, Ephesians 3:20-21)

I decree, declare, and pray that me and my family walk in health and healing. Death and sicknesses are far from each of us in the name of Jesus I pray. (Reference Scriptures: Exodus 23:25, Proverbs 3:7-8, Isaiah 53:5, Isaiah 54:14, Jeremiah 33:6, 1 Corinthians 6:19-20, James 5:14-15, 1 Peter 2:24, 3 John 1:2, Revelation 12:11)

I decree, declare, and pray that my home is a haven for peace in the name of Jesus I pray. (Reference Scriptures: Numbers 6:25-26, Isaiah 26:3, John 14:27, Romans 5:1, Romans 8:6, Romans 14:17-19, Colossians 3:15)

I decree, declare, and pray that my family looks out for the interests of each other sharing with each other in love in the name of Jesus I pray. (Reference Scriptures: Proverbs 20:23, Luke 6:31, Philippians 2:1-5, Hebrews 13:15-16, 1 Timothy 6:17-18)

I decree, declare, and pray that I and my family enjoy keeping God's covenants and commandments with the help of the Holy Spirit in the name of Jesus I pray. (Reference Scriptures: Exodus 20:1-17, Deuteronomy 28: 1-14, Psalms 103:17-18, Isaiah 11:2, John 13:34-35, John 14:15-17, John 14:26, John 16:12-15, Romans 8:26-27, Romans 15:13)

I decree, declare, and pray that as a parent I train, nourish, nurture, instructing my children in the admonition of the Lord without provoking them to anger in the name of Jesus I pray. (Reference Scriptures: Deuteronomy 11:18-22, Deuteronomy 6:5- 7, Psalms 78:5-7, Psalms 127:3, Proverbs 13:24, Proverbs 22:6 & 15, Proverbs 29:15 & 17, Ephesians 6:4, Colossians 3:21, 2 Timothy 2:15, 2 Timothy 3:16)

I decree, declare, and pray that I am spiritually balanced in the name of Jesus I pray. (Reference Scriptures: Proverbs 3:5-6, Romans 12:2, Philippians 4:8 & 11, Ephesians 5:15, 2 Timothy 1:7, Hebrews 11:6, 2 Peter 3:17)

I decree, declare, and pray that I am humble, gentle, and patient and bear with others in love in the name of Jesus I pray. (Reference Scriptures: Proverbs 15:1, Galatians 5:22-23, Ephesians 4:1-3, Philippians 2:1-4, 2 Timothy 2:24-26, Titus 3:2, James 3:17, James 4:6, 1 Peter 5:6)

I decree, declare, and pray that I make every effort to keep the unity of the spirit in the bond of peace with my brethren in the name of Jesus I pray. (Reference Scriptures: Psalms 133:1, Ephesians 4:3)

I decree, declare, and pray that I build myself and others up in love in the name of Jesus I pray. (Reference Scripture: Ephesians 4:16)

I decree, declare, and pray that I am sensitive to the spirit of the Lord and the needs of others in the name of Jesus I pray. (Reference Scriptures: Jude 1:20, Romans 12:16-21, Philippians 2:1-5, James 3:13-18, James 4:1-12)

I decree, declare, and pray that I am wise and understanding, I give no place to the devil in my relationships. No weapon formed against me shall prosper in name of Jesus I pray. (Reference Scriptures: Isaiah 54:17, Ephesians 4:26-27, James 3:13-18, James 4:1-12)

I decree, declare, and pray that I speak wholesome words to others, things that are good for necessary edification, imparting grace to those that hear me in the name of Jesus I pray. (Reference Scripture: Ephesians 4:29)

I decree, declare, and pray that I practice seeing the possibilities, qualities, and God given potential in others in the name of Jesus I pray. (Reference Scriptures: 2 Corinthians 5:17, 1 John 4:4, 1 Peter 2:9)

I decree, declare, and pray that I put into practice daily, working to show others I love them and sincerely care for them in the name of Jesus I pray. (Reference Scriptures: 1 Corinthians 13:1-13)

I decree, declare, and pray that I lift others up for their strengthening, encouragement, comfort, and edification in the name of Jesus I pray. (Reference Scriptures: Proverbs 27:17, 1 Corinthians 14:3, 1 Corinthians 14:26, 1 Thessalonians 5:11, Hebrews 10:24-25, Hebrews 3:13)

I decree, declare, and pray that my speech is gracious and I know how I should answer others in the name of Jesus I pray. (Reference Scripture: Colossians 4:6)

I decree, declare, and pray that I practice loving-kindness and compassion towards others; forgiving others just like God has forgiven me in the name of Jesus I pray. (Reference Scriptures: Proverbs 19:11, Matthew 6:14-15, Mark 11:25, Galatians 6:7, Ephesians 4:32, Colossians 3:12-15, James 1:25, James 4:12)

CHAPTER SEVEN

COMMUNICATIONS
DECREES, DECLARES & PRAYERS

The tongue has the power
of life and death.

Proverbs 18:21

Thou shalt also decree a thing, and it
shall be established unto thee: and
the light shall shine upon thy ways.

Job 22:28

I decree, declare, and pray that every
good and perfect gift comes down from
the Father of light; therefore, today shall
end good and it shall end perfect
in Jesus' name I pray!

James 1:17

Communication begins with values. Jesus said in Matthews 15:10-11 that what comes out of the mouth is what makes us unclean.

I decree, declare, and pray that I purpose and choose to be quick to listen and slow to speak in the name of Jesus I pray. (Reference Scriptures: Proverbs 10:19, Proverbs 17:28, Proverbs 18:13, James 1:19-20)

I decree, declare, and pray that I am moved by the Holy Spirit cultivating my heart towards godliness in creating effective living and witnessing for Christ in all manners of my communication in the name of Jesus I pray. (Reference Scriptures: Psalmss 51:10, Proverbs 25:11, Proverbs 27:19, Colossians 4:6, 1 Peter 3:15, 2 Peter Chapter 1, 2 Peter 3:11, Hebrews 4:12)

I decree, declare, and pray that I communicate information clearly, accurately, and honestly in the name of Jesus I pray. (Reference Scriptures: Leviticus 19:11, Exodus 20:16, Proverbs 12:22, Proverbs 20:11)

I decree, declare, and pray that I practice hearing a matter before responding in the name of Jesus I pray. (Reference Scripture: Proverbs 18:13)

I decree, declare, and pray that I value listening and understanding all matters in the name of Jesus I pray. (Reference Scriptures: Proverbs 2:2, Proverbs 12:15, Proverbs 19:20, Proverbs 25:12, Proverbs 18:2, Philippians 2:4)

I decree, declare, and pray that the words of my mouth and the meditations of my heart will be pleasing in the sight of the Lord in the name of Jesus I pray. (Reference Scripture: Psalms 19:14)

I decree, declare, and pray that I allow the Holy Spirit to keep me calm in all matters and I avoid getting into wrath in all situations in the name of Jesus I pray. (Reference Scriptures: Exodus 14:14, Judges 6:3, Psalms 37:8, Psalms 94:18-19, Psalms 121:1-2, Proverbs 15:18, Proverbs 17:27, Zephaniah 3:17, Matthew 11:28-29, Matthew 6:31-34, Mark 4:39-40, James 1:19)

I decree, declare, and pray that I practice love in all situations in the name of Jesus I pray. (Reference Scriptures: 1 Corinthians 13:4-6)

I decree, declare, and pray that I have a cheerful heart in the name of Jesus I pray. (Reference Scripture: Proverbs 17:22)

I decree, declare, and pray that I practice discernment and discretion in all matters in the name of Jesus I pray. (Reference Scriptures: Proverbs 2:1-5, Proverbs 2:11, Proverbs 3:1-8, 1 John 4:1-3, Hebrews 4:12, Hebrews 5:14, Philippians 1:9-10, 2 Timothy 3:15)

I decree, declare, and pray that I speak graciously toward others in the name of Jesus I pray. (Reference Scripture: Colossians 4:6)

I decree, declare, and pray that I focus my thoughts and harness my words in the name of Jesus I pray. (Reference Scriptures: Deuteronomy 30:19, Proverbs 23:7, Romans 8:6, 2 Timothy 1:7)

I decree, declare, and pray that I am completely humble, gentle, and patient bearing with others in love in the name of Jesus I pray. (Reference Scriptures: Ephesians 4:1-3, 2 Peter 1:1-10)

I decree, declare, and pray that I make every effort to keep and live in the unity of the Spirit through the bond of peace with those in the body of Christ in the name of Jesus I pray. (Reference Scriptures: Psalms 133:1, Ephesians 4:3, 2 Peter 1:1-10)

I decree, declare, and pray that I speak the truth in love in the name of Jesus I pray. (Reference Scripture: Ephesians 4:15)

I decree, declare, and pray that I build myself and others up in love in the name of Jesus I pray. (Reference Scripture: Ephesians 4:16)

I decree, declare, and pray that I always see the possibilities in myself and my God given potential. I can truly see the best in myself and others in the name of Jesus I pray. (Reference Scriptures: Luke 1:37, 2 Corinthians 5:17, 1 John 4:4, 1 Peter 2:9)

I decree, declare, and pray that I am very effective with interpersonal communications. I seek first to understand others then to be understood. I am strengthening the skills of listening and choosing words that nurture and encourage others in the name of Jesus I pray. (Reference Scriptures: Proverbs 12:18, Proverbs 12:25, Ephesians 4:29, 1 Thessalonians 5:11, Hebrews 10:24-25)

I decree, declare, and pray that I am sensitive to the spirit of the Lord and the needs of others in the name of Jesus I pray. (Reference Scriptures: Isaiah 58:6-9, Jude 1:20-21, Romans 12:15-21, Romans 15:1-3, Philippians 2:1-5, James 2:14-16, James 3:13-18, James 4:1-12)

I decree, declare, and pray that I always see the possibilities, qualities, and potential in others in the name of Jesus I pray. (Reference Scriptures: Genesis 18:14, Jeremiah 32:17, Matthew 19:26, 2 Corinthians 5:17, 1 John 4:4, 1 Peter 2:9)

I decree, declare, and pray that I am clothed in the whole armor of God able to stand against the wiles, tricks, and schemes of the devil in the name of Jesus I pray. (Reference Scriptures: Matthew 16:23, 2 Corinthians 2:10-11, Jude 1:9, Ephesians 6:10-18, James 4:7, 1 John 2:16, 1 John 4:1)

I decree, declare, and pray that I refrain from anger and turn from wrath in the name of Jesus I pray. (Reference Scriptures: Psalms 19:14, Psalms 37:8, Proverbs 15:1)

I decree, declare, and pray that my speech, my conversations are full of grace. I work to ensure my talk is wholesome and pure in the name of Jesus I pray. (Reference Scriptures: Psalms 19:14, Ephesians 4:29-31, Philippians 4:4-8, Colossians 4:6)

I decree, declare, and pray that I consistently lift others up for their strengthening, encouragement, comfort, and edification in the name of Jesus I pray. (Reference: Proverbs 27:17, Romans 14:19, 1 Corinthians 8:1, 1 Corinthians 14:3, Ephesians 4:15-16, Colossians 3:16, 1 Thessalonians 5:11, Hebrews 3:13, Hebrews 10:24-25)

CHAPTER EIGHT

YOUR WORDS IMPACT
YOUR WORLD

Christ came to save the world (John 3:17). He came to set captives free, heal the brokenhearted, relieve those who suffered in their mind and bodies. He showed selfless acts of love all the way to the cross and to His resurrection. No deceit was found in his mouth against those who opposed him (Isaiah 53:9, 1 Peter 2:21-23). His agenda was fully met.

As a believer and follower of Jesus, ask yourself the question, "what am I doing daily that's creating and leaving behind a better tomorrow not only for myself but others too?" Since Proverbs 18:21 literally states that, "Death and Life are in the power of the tongue", then shouldn't we as believers and followers of Christ be speaking words that create life? Words that create and leave behind hope, love, joy, peace, happiness, healing, value, worth, God's truth, restoration, encouragement, grace, mercy, and faith. Faith filled words and statements, those make for a better impact in the positive and right direction.

What are you contributing to yourself and to those around you for the kingdom of God as a believer? We each have a mission, an assignment, a task to fulfill. Every day we are creating something and leaving something that either brings life or brings death. Our words spoken are the reflections from our heart and thoughts. Jeremiah 17:9 let's us know that "the heart is deceitful above all things."

As a believer, it's a logical protocol to practice reading, listening, and studying the Word of God for yourself, at least once daily. Furthermore, if you profess to be a Christian and you truly love God and follow Jesus, it's your personal duty to be consistent in building up knowledge of the scriptures in your mind, heart, and spirit. As a matter of fact, it becomes a personal desire to do these things without being told. These simple practices will aid in equipping you in the knowledge of God. The Holy Spirit (if you permit it) will give you wisdom to apply the knowledge of God you learned. However, you have to be the one to <u>make a personal choice/decision to apply</u> what you learned when the Holy Spirit brings the Word to your mind. The Holy Spirit on the inside of you will cause your mind/thoughts to recall what the Word of God says for you to say out loud and do when faced with trails, tribulations, and shortcomings within your life time. This also applies when you are speaking to others or about someone in your conversations.

You are able to address those issues by decreeing, declaring, and praying the Word of God out loud over yourself and others. Hebrews 4:12 states, "For the Word of God is living and powerful, and sharper than any twoedged sword, piercing even to the division of soul and spirit, and of joints and marrow, and is a discerner of the thoughts and intents of the heart."

The Word of God spoken out loud in faith creates impact in our lives, the lives of others, and in the world. Our words come from our thoughts and internal dialog. Therefore, it's a more positive impact if you are full of the Word, able to recall it, and readily to apply it in all situations. Words are so powerful that just by carelessly speaking them they become our reality.

If you combine the Word of God (remember what Hebrews 4:12 says) add your faith to your confessions then your reality will be what you speak and say about yourself because words shape beliefs. Our faith will increase in whatever we choose to hear and believe. People can go through the motions of living a life, but are you living on a positive impact in your home, your church, your school, your community, your state, your country? The Word of God says in 1 Corinthians 2:16 that as a believer we have the mind of Christ. So are you applying His mind to your everyday life? One thing Christ did and still does is He speaks life. His Words are still saving souls, delivering captives, and mending the broken hearts. Hallelujah!

Our words will do the same. God has given us authority through Christ Jesus and the dominion over our world. (Genesis 1:26, and 28, Psalms 8:6, Luke 10:19, Romans 6:14)

Psalms 34:13 advises us, "Keep your tongue from evil, and your lips from speaking deceit." You may not be using profanity, but are you thinking, speaking, and behaving like an unbeliever? Speaking unwholesome words, belittling others, stirring up strife, causing division among people, speaking lies and sowing discord, saying hateful or mean things about people behind their backs or to their face, being a tale bearer (gossiper) about other peoples private matters, thinking and speaking lowly of yourself (low self esteem, low self worth), practicing deception on others to get your way and your wants met (manipulating people to do what you want), taking advantage of the vulnerabilities of others, all these are evil, deceitful and negative. These ALL lead to death and destruction – this is ALL NEGATIVE!

As a professed Christian and believer, we are required and commended to be speaking the Word of God which is truth, life, and it is all positive.

The Word of God is clear in Hebrews 11:1, "Now faith is the substance of things hoped for, the evidence of things not seen." See with your spiritual eyes, speak the Word with faith, call those things that be not the way God's principles instructs us to speak and live. If you practice life giving words, then you will impact this world in a positive way!

CHAPTER NINE

INVEST IN YOURSELF
INVESTMENTS PAY OFF

Investments have payoffs. Good investments or bad investments, there's always a payoff. Spend some of your money and time investing in yourself. Start with these decrees, declares, and prayers. You have this book, so use it daily and share it with others.

Read the Bible for yourself, buy the Bible on CD's, DVD's, and/or download it from the Internet for your computer or mobile devices. Just get the Word on the inside of you because it's that powerful! (Hebrews 4:12)

Watch and take notes of things happening in you and around you. God has a purpose for each one of us to fulfill regardless of where we have come from or find ourselves now. He has allowed us the gift of free will to choose and make our own decisions. He highly suggests that we choose life! (Deuteronomy 30:19)

As a believer in Christ Jesus, we each have been predestined for something marvelous, but we also have the gift of a free will to choose if we want to live in that marvelous! It starts with our words we choose to speak. What are you confessing? We are all created in the image and "likeness" of God;

therefore, if we really want what God wants for us, then we must practice walking and talking like God. Amen!

His Holy Spirit will lead, guide, and instruct <u>if you ask</u> for help. It's not about denying your circumstances or ignoring warnings, it's about going to the Word of God and choosing to speak out loud what He has said over you as His child. Then, as a child of God apply His Word to everything!

2 Corinthians 4:7 says that "we have this treasure in earthen vessels that the excellence of the power may be of God and not of us." "The excellence of the power may be of God and not of us," that's what happens when you choose God's Words and practice God's way of speaking and handling matters while denying your own fleshly desires and deny following the traditions of men.

It may be your family tradition to speak negatively about yourself, others, and situations, but that is not God's way.

God's Word, once again, says in Proverbs 18:21 that "THE TONGUE HAS THE POWER OF LIFE AND DEATH, AND THOSE THAT LOVE IT WILL EAT ITS FRUIT." Therefore, whatever you are saying about YOURSELF AND OTHERS, you are going to eat the fruit of your lips! You will get what you speak, it will be your reality, it will continue to be your circumstances.

Why not choose life giving words, positive words, and speak the Word of God over your circumstances? Watch and see God show you that this really does work in your favor and for His glory!

<u>Let no unwholesome words proceed out of your mouth</u>

(corrupt communications) except those words that edify (encourage, lift, and build up) so those words will minister grace to the hearers. (Ephesians 4:29 AMP) The definitions for the word "grace" are: a pleasing and charming quality, an unmerited gift, to honor or favor.

So ask yourself if you are ministering grace with your words to yourself and others? CHOOSE to read OUT LOUD some of these decrees, declares, and prayers over your life daily. Pray the prayers consistently out loud. God hears what we say and keeps a record. Not only will you see God at work to perform His Word, people around you will see God at work.

Most of us have all heard that misery loves company, well the opposite of that is also true. We all feel good or better when someone speaks graciously to us. We all enjoy being around happy, charismatic, loving, optimistic, and positive people. Invest in yourself daily by choosing to speak life giving words. This investment in yourself and others will pay off in the best way possible. Read your Bible daily. Put the Word of God in practice daily. Read this book periodically for yourself and please share it with others.

Choose Life Giving Words!

So, let's get to work! God is in a hurry to transform lives for His glory and for His kingdom purposes. This is a valuable investment with the greatest payoff for mankind – especially a believer of Christ!

KEEP THIS IN MIND:

Routine creates consistency. Consistency creates instinct behavior. Create your verbal routine to express truth, optimism, joy, grace, love, kindness, compassion, charity, hope, health, wellness, and good will towards your own life. God will then use you effectively to express His character and demonstrate His principles to those you come in contact with during the course of your life.

Proverbs 18:21 provides insight to creating life (The tongue has the power of life and death). Philippians 4:8 provides instructions for our minds (Finally, brethren, whatever things are true, whatever things are noble, whatever things are just, whatever things are pure, whatever things are lovely, whatever things are of good report, if there is any virtue and if there is anything praiseworthy, meditate on these things).

Feed your mind and spirit with the Word of God so you will automatically choose to speak kingdom words, make faith filled statements, and spread life giving words.

Your mouth will automatically create a powerful life worth living!

ABOUT THE AUTHOR

Caroline Green enjoys sharing divine wisdom, divine insight, and God's revelation knowledge in order to educate, empower, and encourage others. Especially those in the household of faith.

Caroline loves prayer and knows the power of prayer. To learn more about Caroline Green, please visit www.carolinegreen.org, or follow her Author's Page on Amazon, connect through social media outlets such as, Facebook, Twitter, Periscope, or YouTube.

ONE LAST THING

Have you enjoyed any part of this book or found it useful? I personally wrote this book with my own two hands and 10 fingers. No ghostwriters here! It has taken a few years to complete. Therefore, I would be honored for your support in submitting a positive review and post a short statement on Amazon.

Your support really does make a difference! I read reviews for inspiration and motivation to keep pressing forward!
To leave a review, all you need to do is click the review link on this book's page on Amazon.

Thanks so much for your reviews, prayers, and support!

My prayer for all the readers:

May the Lord bless you, keep you, and make His face shine upon you, and be gracious to you. May the Lord lift up His countenance upon you and give you peace. In the mighty name of Jesus I pray. Amen!

Caroline Green

WRITE YOUR OWN
DECREES, DECLARES & PRAYERS

WRITE YOUR OWN
DECREES, DECLARES & PRAYERS

WRITE YOUR OWN
DECREES, DECLARES & PRAYERS

WRITE YOUR OWN
DECREES, DECLARES & PRAYERS

Made in the USA
San Bernardino, CA
02 January 2020

62605192R00093